GREEK COOKING

GREEK
COOKING

Lou Seibert Pappas

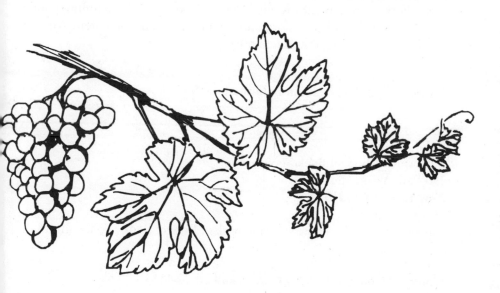

GALAHAD BOOKS
New York

First Galahad Books edition published in 1995.

Galahad Books
A division of Budget Book Service, Inc.
386 Park Avenue South
New York, NY 10016

Galahad Books is a registered trademark of Budget Book Service, Inc.

Library of Congress Catalog Card Number: 73-4115

ISBN: 0-88365-893-3

Printed in the United States of America.

To Yaya and Papou
  Panayiota and Leonidas Papamihalópoulos

CONTENTS

Dining in Greece

Greece and its isles, a land of brilliant blue skies and sparkling pure seas, offer a tantalizing cuisine, beloved by its discoverers. The Greek's zest for the good life and his innate love of fine, simple foods is reflected at his table. The warmth, hospitality, and spirit of the people characterize their cuisine as well. It is a cuisine that is delicately spiced, robust, and intricately varied. In the villages especially, the table is cyclical, changing as the seasons unfurl, bringing a chain of color and beauty.

The land, cleansed by sun and sea wind, offers a variety of fresh ingredients close at hand. The azure seas are blessed with an abundance of fish and shellfish. Olive trees flourish, providing a flavor-packed oil in which to bathe other foods. Vineyards thread the rolling hills, and the grape crush and ferment produce excellent wines, some resin-flavored. Fragrant lemon trees bend at every door, bearing the golden fruit for *avgolemono*, the refreshing lemon sauce whose tang pervades Greek gastronomy.

Lamb is the principal meat served. A holiday festivity calls for ceremoniously spit-roasting a whole carcass out of doors, but for everyday meals, lamb is braised in stews or casseroles with every conceivable vegetable, and skewered and broiled lamb is popularly sold by street vendors throughout Greece. Chicken is broiled or braised, or stuffed whole with an unusual chestnut dressing and roasted. Mountain-grown herbs—garlic, oregano, mint, basil, and dill—and freshly ground cinnamon sticks and nutmegs season these fragrant meat and poultry dishes. But even today, meat is scarce in villages still by-passed by roads, and the morning's catch provides the daily fare instead.

Greek food is designed to be made in advance and served warm or tepid. The villagers are accustomed to preparing a single dish in great quantity for several meals, and in the country and island villages one always sees bare-legged young boys or shawled, time-worn matriarchs carrying a great panful of moussaka or *pastitsio* to the local baker for a crusting over in the brick oven.

Good meat and vegetable combinations are countless. They might pair braised lamb or veal with greens or arti-choke hearts in *avgolemono*; or chicken and zucchini in a caramelized onion and tomato sauce; or beef or hare and tiny boiling onions in a cinnamon-spiced tomato sauce, named *stifado*. Moussaka, layered with eggplant or zuc-chini and spicy garlic-scented meat sauce, and wearing a golden custard topping, is a ubiquitous casserole dish, and the fascinating fila pitas, layered with chicken and mush-rooms, or lamb and leeks, or feta and spinach, are a delight.

An abundance of fresh vegetables—artichokes, carrots, eggplant, cabbage, green beans, onions, zucchini, and both cultivated and wild greens—inspires imaginative cooked and marinated vegetable dishes and salads. Rounds of cheese—fresh feta, Romano, and Kasseri, in particular—are used lavishly, either sliced to accompany homemade whole wheat bread or salad, or grated and used to top vegetables or pasta tossed in browned butter.

Appetizers play an important role in the Greek kitchen, reflecting the Greek's enjoyment of a leisurely and friendly hour of socializing before the late dinner is served. The *taverna* comes to life as the day's work ends. Here Greeks gather to sip ouzo or wine and savor *meze*, or appetizers, meaning "something to whet the appetite." These include many shapes and hues of olives, cheeses, pickled vegetables, bite-sized meatballs, stuffed grape leaves, crispy fried octopus or shrimp, and the marvelous fila-wrapped savories, containing feta, meat sauce, or spinach mixtures. *Taramosalata*, piped in a ribbon or swirled into a pyramid, is a prize spread on the crusty soft bread.

Soups and breads are closely allied with holidays. Greeks break the Lenten fast with *Mageritsa*, an egg-and-lemon-thickened broth brewed with lamb innards. Lentil soup is traditional fare on Holy Friday. Christmas, New Year's, and Easter each have their specialty yeast breads, imbued with spices and shaped in particular designs.

Undoubtedly, the most celebrated specialty of the Greek kitchen is that remarkable pastry called fila or phyllo. This tissue-thin dough is as fine as onionskin. It is the crispy foundation for countless appetizers, vegetable dishes, entrées, and innumerable pastries.

A visit to a Greek pastry shop, or *zacharopleasteai*, reveals the versatility of fila dough. There one discovers several dozen different fila pastries, many of Turkish derivation. The most internationally famous dessert is baklava, a multilayered fila pastry ribboned with nuts and oozing with honey syrup. Other names are colorful and poetic, with down-to-earth translations. *Hanoum*, the Turkish word for "woman," is a large spiral-shaped, almond-filled baklava. Istanbul flute is a slender nut-filled cylinder about six inches long. *Kadaife* from Yanina has fila leaves rolled around the shredded *kadaife* dough, and it looks very much like the flute version. *Kourkabounia* means "from a tree," an apt label, for coconut twirls inside its fila. *Saraglakia* has almonds encased within. *Bougatsa* is a neat rectangular fila package sealing inside an orange liqueur-scented farina custard. *Svoloti* are fruit-filled fila rolls, adorned with pistachios.

Baklava is cut in triangles as well as diamonds and composed of various nuts or nut combinations. There are triangles of *trigona* and thick diamonds of *kopehagi,* whose almond soufflé center rests on a sheet of pound cake between fila.

Besides the fila pastries, there are other sweets. *Milopita* and *karithopita* are individual apple and walnut scalloped tarts. *Touloumpes* is a blimp-shaped Istanbul doughnut— light, eggy, and delectable. *Spholiates* is a flaky pastry filled with nuts and fruits. *Pastaflora* has dried apricots, figs, and raisins centered in its golden cake square.

There are also delicious Greek-style croissants. These fat crescents are rolled up with strawberry jam and chopped walnuts. Other yeast buns are filled with ground walnuts and sugar and drizzled with powdered sugar frosting. The hot feta cheese buns, resembling a big flat piroshki, are a swift-selling morning snack.

Cookies are called *koutima. Theples* from Filiatra are deep-fried twisted knots, encased in syrup. *Koulourakia* come in half a dozen or more assorted shapes. Nut macaroons are big, and a pretty sight with an apricot glaze and a shower of green pistachios. Sandwich cookies are stuck together with marmalade or apricot preserves between and nuts or seeds on top. The gaudy cakes are best passed up.

The honeyed fila pastries and buttery nut cookies compose a separate late afternoon meal accompanied by thick Greek coffee or wine and folk music. Fresh fruit—figs, oranges, apples, and melon—usually concludes the late evening dinner.

Feasts and festival are integral to Hellenic life. Name days, saints' days, weddings, and holidays are the occasion for merriment—a bounteous table and spirited folk dancing.

Menus for All Occasions

🦂 BRUNCH FOR A CROWD

Cantaloupe with Strawberries
Feta Cheese Omelet (optional)
Ham-Filled Pie
Honey Coffee Bread
Greek Coffee

🦂 WEEKEND LUNCH FOR GUESTS

Olives/Cheeses/Cherry Tomatoes
Cucumber and Yogurt Salad
Chicken Pita or Pastitsio
Yogurt Cake

🦂 MAKE-AHEAD FAMILY DINNER

Tomatoes with Feta Dressing
Beef and Onion Stew
Pilaf with Fides
Kasseri and Winter Pears

🐾 SUNDAY FAMILY DINNER

> Meze: Parsley Meatballs/Olives
> Marinated Mushrooms/Cheeses/Celery
> Roast Chicken Plaka Style
> Braised Green Beans
> Almond Soufflé Pastry

🐾 SUMMER GARDEN PARTY

> Shrimp Plaka Style
> Avgolemono Soup
> Beef Fila Rolls
> Cheese Fila Rolls
> Skewered Dolmathes and Cherry Tomatoes
> Asparagus with Kasseri
> Lemon Ice in Cantaloupe Shells

🐾 DINNER PARTY WITH SURPRISES

> Arab Bread
> Eggplant Salad
> Lamb Bandit Style
> Orange Nut Crêpes

🐾 SIT-DOWN DINNER FOR EIGHT

> Taramosalata with Cucumbers
> Wreath Bread
> Green Salad with Feta
> Roast Lamb with Artichokes
> Pilaf
> Galatoboureko   Strawberries

❧ CLASSIC GREEK DINNER

Avgolemono Soup
Country Salad
Moussaka
Roast Chicken
Almond Cake

❧ OUTDOOR MEZE PARTY

Feta, Kasseri, and Olives
Sesame Seed Spread with Wreath Bread
Parsley Meatballs
Stuffed Mussels
Spinach and Cheese Pitas
Crab and Mushroom Marinated Salad
Saragli (optional)
Halvah   Strawberries
Retsina   Turkish Coffee

❧ EASTER DINNER IN THE GARDEN

Meze: Feta, Kasseri, Olives, Taramosalata
Basket of Red Eggs
Easter Twist
Spinach and Feta Salad
Kid on a Spit, or Roast Leg of Lamb
Pilaf
Artichokes à la Constantinople
Easter Shortbread Cookies
Baklava   Strawberries

🦁 SUMMER BUFFET PARTY

Yogurt Soup
Avocado with Taramosalata
Chicken with Skordalia Sauce
Steamed Summer Squash
Walnut Cake
Basket of Cherries and Apricots

🦁 CHRISTMAS DINNER

Cheese Triangles   Meat Triangles
Feta   Kasseri   Pistachios
Christmas Bread
Country Salad
Roast Stuffed Turkey
Whole Cauliflower with Artichokes
Sweet Potatoes or Yams
Kourabiedes   Baklava
Nut Pastry Flutes

GREEK COOKING

APPETIZERS

These multilayered cheese pastries freeze beautifully after being baked. The secret to their triangular shape is folding fila strips like a flag. Pronounce the name tee-RO-peetas. Prepared fila dough is available in some delicatessens and Greek markets in one-pound packages.

Cheese Triangles / *Tiropetes*

    1 pound feta cheese
    1 pound ricotta cheese, or ½ pound *each* cottage
       cheese and cream cheese
    3 eggs
    3 tablespoons finely chopped fresh parsley
    Dash pepper
    ½ pound prepared fila dough
    ¾ cup butter, melted

Place the cheeses, eggs, parsley, and pepper in a mixing bowl and beat until well blended.

Lay out one sheet of fila at a time (keep remaining fila covered with clear plastic film), and cut into strips 3 inches wide and about 12 inches long. Brush each strip lightly with melted butter. Place a rounded teaspoon of the cheese filling on one end of fila strip, and fold over one corner to make a triangle. Continue folding pastry from side to side, making a triangle (like folding a flag). Place on a lightly buttered baking sheet. Proceed in this manner, making pastry triangles with remaining fila and filling. Brush tops of triangles with melted butter.

Bake in a 350° oven for 15 minutes, or until golden brown. Serve hot. If desired, let cool and freeze, wrapped airtight. To serve later, let thaw and reheat at 350° for 15 minutes, or until hot through and crispy. Makes about 8 dozen.

A sprightly beef and walnut sauce makes plump cushions inside crispy fila triangles.

Meat Triangles / *Kreatopetes*

1 medium-sized onion, finely chopped
¾ cup butter
2 pounds lean ground beef
¼ cup tomato paste
½ cup dry red wine
2 cloves garlic, minced
1½ teaspoons salt
Freshly ground pepper
⅓ cup freshly grated Parmesan cheese
2 eggs
2 tablespoons fine dry bread crumbs
⅓ cup chopped walnuts or pistachios (optional)
½ pound prepared fila dough

Using a large frying pan, sauté onion in 2 tablespoons of the butter until golden brown. Push to sides of pan, add meat, and brown until crumbly, stirring. Add tomato paste, wine, garlic, salt, and pepper. Cover and simmer for 20 minutes. Remove cover and cook down quickly until meat sauce is thickened. Remove from heat and let cool. Mix in cheese, eggs, crumbs, and nuts, if desired.

Melt remaining butter. Lay out one sheet of fila at a time (keep remaining fila covered with clear plastic film), and cut into strips 3 inches wide and about 12 inches long. Brush each strip lightly with melted butter. Place a rounded teaspoon of meat filling on one end of fila strip and fold over one corner to make a triangle. Continue folding pastry from side to side, making a triangle. Place on a lightly buttered baking sheet. Proceed in this manner, making pastry triangles with remaining fila and filling. Brush tops of triangles with melted butter. Bake in a 350° oven for 15 minutes, or until golden brown. Serve hot.

If desired, let cool and freeze, wrapped airtight. To serve later, let thaw and reheat at 350° for 15 minutes, or until hot through and crispy. Makes about 8 dozen.

Fresh chopped spinach and three cheeses puff within fila wrappers.

Spinach Triangles / *Spanakopetes*

>   1 bunch green onions, finely chopped
>   ¼ cup olive oil
>   1 pound fresh spinach, washed and finely chopped
>   ½ pound ricotta cheese or cream cheese
>   ½ pound feta cheese
>   2 eggs
>   ⅓ cup fine dry bread crumbs
>   ½ cup freshly grated Parmesan cheese
>   Dash pepper
>   3 tablespoons finely chopped fresh parsley
>   ⅛ teaspoon nutmeg
>   ½ pound prepared fila dough
>   ¾ cup butter, melted

In a large frying pan sauté onions in oil until limp. Add spinach and cook over medium high heat just until limp. Remove from heat and let cool slightly. Beat together ricotta or cream cheese, feta, eggs, bread crumbs, Parmesan, pepper, parsley, and nutmeg. Mix in sautéed vegetables.

Lay out one sheet of fila at a time (keep remaining fila covered with clear plastic film), and cut into strips 3 inches wide and about 12 inches long. Brush each strip lightly with melted butter. Place a rounded teaspoon of spinach-cheese filling on one end of fila strip and fold over one corner. Continue folding from side to side, making a triangle. Place on a lightly buttered baking sheet. Proceed in this manner, making pastry triangles with remaining fila and filling. Brush tops of triangles with melted butter.

Bake in a 350° oven for 15 minutes, or until golden brown. Serve hot. If desired, let cool and freeze, wrapped airtight. To serve later, let thaw and reheat at 350° for 15 minutes, or until hot through and crispy. Makes about 8 dozen.

🦂

Other fresh or canned seafood, such as lobster or Dungeness or Alaska King crab meat can substitute for shrimp in these neat fila packages.

Shellfish Triangles / *Psaropetes*

½ pound cream cheese
2 egg yolks
2 tablespoons finely chopped fresh parsley
2 green onions, finely chopped
1 teaspoon lemon juice
½ teaspoon Worcestershire sauce
¼ teaspoon salt
1 cup small cooked shrimp, chopped
⅓ cup freshly grated Parmesan cheese
8 sheets (approximately) prepared fila dough
6 tablespoons butter, melted

Beat the cheese until creamy and mix in egg yolks, parsley, onions, lemon juice, Worcestershire, salt, shrimp, and Parmesan. Beat until blended.

Lay out one sheet of fila at a time (keep remaining fila covered with clear plastic film) and cut into strips 3 inches wide and about 12 inches long. Brush each strip lightly with melted butter. Place a rounded teaspoon of cheese filling on one end of fila strip and fold over one corner to make a triangle. Continue folding pastry from side to side, making a triangle. Place on a lightly buttered baking sheet. Proceed in this manner, making pastry triangles with remaining fila and filling. Brush tops of triangles with melted butter.

Bake in a 350° oven for 15 minutes, or until golden brown. Serve hot. If desired, let cool and freeze, wrapped airtight. To serve later let thaw and reheat at 350° for 15 minutes, or until hot through and crispy. Makes about 4 dozen.

Another way of folding fila strips for appetizers is like a jelly roll with sides tucked in first. Four kinds of cheese blend in these fila rolls. They freeze well, too. It is easy to transform these appetizer rolls into large entrée-size packets, instead. Simply use a full sheet of fila for each one.

Cheese Rolls / *Bourekakia*

1 pound cream cheese
1 pound (1 pint) cottage cheese or ricotta cheese
1 cup freshly grated Parmesan cheese
1½ cups shredded Gruyère, Samsoe, or Swiss cheese
3 eggs
3 tablespoons finely chopped fresh parsley
Salt and freshly ground pepper
24 sheets prepared fila dough
Melted butter or olive oil

In a large mixing bowl beat together the cheeses, eggs, parsley, and salt and pepper to taste.

Lay out the fila sheets flat and cut in half, making rect-angles approximately 9 by 12 inches. Stack fila and cover with clear plastic film. Lay out one piece of fila at a time and brush half of it with melted butter or oil. Fold in half, making about a 6-by-9-inch rectangle. Brush again with butter or oil. Spoon a heaping tablespoon of cheese mix-ture along a narrow end of dough. Fold in sides 1 inch and roll up. Place seam side down on a buttered baking sheet. Repeat. Brush rolls with butter.

Bake in a 350° oven for 20 minutes, or until golden brown. Let cool slightly on racks. If desired, cool and freeze, covered. To serve, let thaw and reheat in a 350° oven for 20 minutes, or until hot through. Makes about 4 dozen appetizers.

ENTRÉE-SIZE VARIATION. Using 16 to 18 sheets fila instead of 24, lay out one sheet of fila at a time, brush half with melted butter or oil, and fold over half to make ap-proximately a 9-by-12-inch rectangle. Brush again with butter. Spoon about ⅓ cup cheese mixture along a narrow end of dough. Fold in sides 1 inch and roll up. Repeat and bake for 25 minutes as di-rected above.

A selection of both cheese and meat rolls makes a winning party buffet entrée.

Meat Rolls / *Bourekakia me Kreas*

> 2 quarts meat sauce (see page 119)
> ¼ cup fine dry bread crumbs
> ¾ cup freshly grated Parmesan cheese
> 3 eggs
> 2 tablespoons finely chopped fresh parsley
> ¼ cup chopped walnuts or whole pine nuts (optional)
> 24 sheets prepared fila dough
> Melted butter or olive oil

Make meat sauce and let cool.

Using a large mixing bowl, mix together the meat sauce, crumbs, cheese, eggs, parsley, and nuts.

Lay out the fila sheets flat and cut in half, making rectangles approximately 9 by 12 inches. Stack fila and cover with clear plastic film. Lay out one piece of fila at a time and brush half of it with melted butter. Fold in half, making about a 6-by-9-inch rectangle. Brush again with butter or oil. Spoon a heaping tablespoon of meat sauce mixture along a narrow end of dough. Fold in sides 1 inch and roll up. Place seam side down on a buttered baking sheet. Repeat. Brush rolls with butter.

Bake in a 350° oven for 20 minutes, or until golden brown. Let cool slightly on racks. If desired, cool and freeze, covered. To serve, let thaw and reheat in a 350° oven for 20 minutes, or until hot through. Makes about 4 dozen appetizers.

ENTRÉE-SIZE VARIATION. Using 16 to 18 sheets fila instead of 24, lay out one sheet of fila at a time, brush half with melted butter, and fold over half to make approximately a 9-by-12-inch rectangle. Brush again with butter. Spoon about ⅓ cup meat sauce mixture along a narrow end of dough. Fold in sides 1 inch and roll up. Repeat and bake for 25 minutes as directed above.

🥢

Lemon-scented stuffed grape leaves make a zestful appetizer or accompaniment to garnish the dinner plate. Let them nestle into pilaf or embellish a platter of grilled fish steaks.

Stuffed Grape Leaves / *Dolmadakia*

1 jar grape leaves (about 3 to 4 dozen) or fresh grape leaves
1 large onion, finely chopped
½ cup olive oil
1 cup short-grain rice
¼ cup finely chopped fresh parsley
2 tablespoons fresh chopped dill, or 1½ teaspoons dried dill
½ teaspoon salt
¼ cup pine nuts
¼ cup currants
6 tablespoons lemon juice
1½ cups beef stock
Lemon wedges

Remove grape leaves from the jar, scald with hot water, and drain. (Or blanch fresh grape leaves in hot water for 1 minute, lift out with a slotted spoon and drain.) Cut off stems from leaves and pat each leaf dry with paper towels. In a large frying pan, sauté onion in 4 tablespoons of the oil until golden. Add rice, parsley, dill, salt, pine nuts, and currants, and 1 cup water. Cover and simmer 10 minutes, or until the liquid is absorbed; let cool.

When cool, place 1 teaspoon of the rice mixture in the center of each leaf (shiny surface down), fold like an envelope, and roll up. (Do not roll too tightly, as rice will expand.) Arrange rolls in layers in a large Dutch oven. Sprinkle with lemon juice and remaining olive oil. Pour beef stock and 1 cup water over rolls. Weight with a baking dish. Cover and simmer for 35 minutes, or until rice is tender. Let cool in pan. Serve chilled, garnished with lemon wedges. Makes 3 to 4 dozen appetizers.

The hinged shells of mussels or clams provide an artistic serving container for seafood pilaf. Chilled, they are an intriguing appetizer or first course; hot, they are a conversational entrée.

Stuffed Mussels / *Midia Yemista*

    2 dozen mussels or clams (little neck or rock)
    ½ cup dry white wine
    ½ cup water
    Salt
    1 large onion, finely chopped

⅓ cup olive oil
1 cup short-grain rice
⅓ cup pine nuts
⅓ cup tomato sauce
¼ cup whole allspice
⅓ cup currants
Lemon wedges

Scrub mussels or clams thoroughly under cold running water, using a stiff brush. Place in a kettle, pour the wine and the water over them, and sprinkle lightly with salt. Cover and steam for 10 minutes, or until the shells open. Reserve broth, strain, and measure. If necessary add enough water to make 1 cup liquid. Discard unopened mussels.

Sauté onion in oil until golden. Add rice and pine nuts, and sauté, stirring, until nuts turn golden brown. Pour the 1 cup reserved liquid over the rice mixture. Add tomato sauce, allspice, and currants. Cover and bring to a boil, reduce heat to low, and let simmer 12 minutes. Remove from heat and let stand 10 minutes. Chop mussels or clams coarsely, then combine with rice and spoon into shells. Cover and chill. Serve cold with lemon wedges. Fills about 2 dozen shells, or enough for 24 appetizers or 6 entrée servings.

Orange peel scents these fat sausage links, wafting a refreshing aroma as they sauté. Buy the sausage casings, about one inch in diameter, at a meat market that specializes in making sausages.

Greek Sausages / *Loukanika*

1½ pounds ground pork
1½ pounds ground veal
1 teaspoon cinnamon
1 teaspoon allspice
1 tablespoon salt
3 cloves garlic, minced
3 tablespoons orange zest, finely chopped (see below) 6 to 8 whole black peppercorns, cracked
¾ cup dry white wine
Sausage casings
1 to 2 tablespoons butter

Mix together the ground meats, cinnamon, allspice, salt, garlic, orange zest, peppercorns, and wine. Using a pastry bag or cookie press, fill the sausage casings with the meat mixture. Tie off links with a clean string, making two ties at each division between links, or twist casing to make links.

To cook sausage links, cut off the number desired, arrange in a frying pan, and cover with hot water. Simmer gently for 20 minutes; drain. Then sauté in 1 to 2 tablespoons butter, turning to brown evenly. Or slice parboiled links ½ inch thick and sauté in butter, turning to brown both sides. Makes about 3 pounds sausage links.

ORANGE ZEST. Use a vegetable peeler to peel off the thin outer orange skin into strips; then chop finely.

These piquant bite-size meatballs can be shaped into large ovals for an entrée as well. This beloved family dish has many variations. Fresh chopped spinach, mint, or grated carrot is sometimes blended into the meat mixture, or lemon juice may replace the vinegar.

Parsley Meatballs / *Keftethes*

1 medium-sized onion, finely chopped
2 tablespoons olive oil
2 tablespoons butter
1 cup soft white bread crumbs
½ cup water
3 egg yolks
2 cloves garlic, peeled
2 teaspoons salt
½ teaspoon dried oregano
3 tablespoons finely chopped fresh parsley
2 pounds lean ground beef
3 tablespoons red wine vinegar
Freshly ground pepper
Oregano

Sauté onion in part of the oil and butter until onion is soft; empty into a mixing bowl. Add bread crumbs, water, egg yolks, garlic, salt, ½ teaspoon oregano, and parsley, and mix well. Add ground beef and mix thoroughly. Shape into balls about 1 inch in diameter. (Or for an entrée, shape into oval mounds about 3 inches long.) Sauté the meatballs in the remaining oil and butter, turning to brown all sides. Transfer to a serving dish. Pour vinegar into the cooking pan, and bring to a boil, scraping up drippings; pour over meatballs. Grind fresh pepper over meatballs, and sprinkle lightly with oregano. Makes about 3 dozen appetizer meatballs.

Quantity Tip. When making a double or triple batch of meatballs for a party, it is easier to bake them instead of frying them. Shape meatballs and place 1 inch apart on a lightly greased baking sheet. Bake at 425° for 20 minutes, or until cooked through. In a small saucepan boil vinegar until reduced by half, add pan drippings from the baked meatballs, and heat until blended. Place meatballs in a serving dish, and pour the sauce over them.

In autumn either freshly gathered chestnuts or those purchased from a market may be shelled and toasted for this hot nutmeat snack.

Roast Chestnuts / *Kastana Psita*

Make two cross-cut gashes on the flat side of the chestnuts with a sharp-pointed knife. Spread out in a single layer in a shallow baking pan and sprinkle lightly with water. Roast in a 375° oven for 10 minutes, or until the shells and inner skin come off. Or place gashed nuts in a wire basket and roast over the coals of a fireplace or barbecue fire until the shells and skin flake off easily. Pass while still warm.

A *smooth canned paste of sesame seeds, called* tahini, *flavors this garbanzo bean spread. It looks dramatic shaped into a pyramid to pile on* lavosh *or tuck inside wedges of hot pita bread. The spread is actually Arabic in origin.*

Sesame Spread / *Hummus Tahini*

> 1 can (1 pound) garbanzo beans, drained
> ⅓ cup lemon juice
> ½ cup *tahini* paste
> 3 tablespoons chopped green onion
> 2 cloves garlic, peeled
> Salt and pepper
> Cilantro or parsley sprigs
> *Lavosh* (cracker bread) or Arabic bread

Place the beans in a blender container with lemon juice, *tahini,* onion, and garlic, and blend until smooth. Add salt and pepper to taste, and blend again. Empty into a bowl, cover, and chill. When ready to serve, mound in a pyramid on a small serving plate and garnish with a wreath of cilantro or parsley sprigs. Spread on *lavosh* or Arabic bread. Makes about 2 cups.

🦋

Mushrooms simmer in an oil and lemon bath, thus retaining their whiteness and absorbing a tantalizing herb bouquet.

Marinated Mushrooms / *Manitaria Marinata*

> ⅓ cup water
> ¼ cup olive oil
> 3 tablespoons lemon juice
> 1 bay leaf

1 clove garlic, minced
4 peppercorns
¼ teaspoon dried tarragon or thyme
1 pound small button mushrooms, cleaned and
   trimmed
1 tablespoon finely chopped chives or parsley

In a large frying pan place ⅓ cup water and the oil, lemon juice, bay leaf, garlic, peppercorns, and tarragon or thyme. Bring to a boil, add mushrooms, cover, and simmer 3 minutes. With a slotted spoon, remove mushrooms from pan and place in a serving dish. Quickly boil down pan juices until reduced by half, and spoon over mushrooms; chill. Before serving, sprinkle with chives or parsley. Serve with toothpicks, or on an appetizer plate with forks. Makes about 8 to 10 appetizer servings.

Wine-kissed shrimp, redolent with garlic, are excellent as an appetizer or entrée. Crusty chunks of kouloura *are just right for sponging up the pan juices.*

Shrimp Plaka Style / *Garides a la Plaka*

2 pounds extra-large raw shrimp, peeled and
   deveined (12 count to a pound)
½ cup olive oil or butter
½ cup dry white wine
¼ cup lemon juice
3 cloves garlic, minced
1 teaspoon dried oregano
3 tablespoons finely chopped fresh parsley
Salt and pepper

Arrange shrimp in a large shallow baking dish. In a sauce-pan combine the oil or butter, wine, lemon juice, garlic, oregano, parsley, and salt and pepper to taste. Heat just until boiling, and pour over the shrimp. Bake in a 375° oven for 15 minutes, or until shrimp turn pink. Serve from the baking dish, or transfer to a large platter and spoon over the sauce. Have a basket of crusty bread alongside. Serve on small plates with forks. Makes about 2 dozen appetizer servings or 4 entrée servings.

🦎

This fish roe mayonnaise has many serving possibilities. Use as a spread for sesame crackers, a dip for raw vegetables, or a topping for cherry tomatoes. Or mound it inside avocado half-shells for a striking first-course plate.

Fish Roe Spread / *Taramosalata*

2 slices white bread, crusts removed
4-ounce jar tarama (carp roe) or red caviar
⅓ cup lemon juice
¼ cup chopped green onions (both white and
   green parts)
1 cup olive oil, or ½ cup *each* olive oil and salad
   oil
Salt and pepper
Finely chopped fresh parsley or cilantro
Sesame crackers, *lavosh* (cracker bread), or
Arabic bread

Place the bread, tarama or caviar, lemon juice, and onions in a blender container and blend a few seconds. With motor running, gradually pour in the oil, blending until thick and creamy. Add salt and pepper to taste, and blend again. Empty into a bowl and chill. Sprinkle with parsley or cilantro just before serving. Spread on crackers or bread. Makes about 2 cups.

SOUPS

This famous soup is simply a bond of broth, eggs, and lemon juice. It comes in infinite variation. Basic proportions are 1 cup broth, 1 egg, and 1 tablespoon lemon juice. The eggs may be separated and beaten separately, giving a frothy effect. Heavy cream may be added for a velvety texture. Or for a make-ahead version, cornstarch may be blended with cold water and stirred into the hot broth to prevent curdling.

Lemon Soup / *Avgolemono*

> 4 cups rich chicken broth
> 4 eggs
> 4 tablespoons lemon juice
> 1 whole lemon, thinly sliced

Heat chicken broth to boiling. In a large mixing bowl, beat eggs with a wire whisk until light, and beat in the lemon juice. Gradually stir in half the broth, whisking constantly. Return to saucepan and place over low heat until soup is thickened, stirring frequently. Pour into small cups and garnish with a lemon slice. Makes 8 first-course servings.

FROTHY VARIATION. Heat stock to boiling. Separate eggs; beat egg yolks with lemon juice until blended. Beat egg whites until soft peaks form, and fold in yolk mixture. Gradually stir in half the broth, whisking. Return to saucepan and place over low heat, stirring, until thickened.

CREAMY VARIATION. Pour ½ cup heavy cream into the finished soup, stirring constantly, and serve at once.

MAKE-AHEAD VARIATION. Heat chicken broth to boiling. Blend 2 tablespoons cornstarch with 2 tablespoons cold water and stir into the boiling broth. Continue as directed in basic recipe.

🐝

This is a full-meal soup, perfect with crusty bread and sliced cucumbers and tomatoes dashed with olive oil and crumbled feta.

Meatball Soup / *Youvarlakia Soupa*

1½ pounds ground veal, lamb, or beef
1 small onion, grated
2 tablespoons minced parsley
¼ cup rice
1 teaspoon salt
2 cloves garlic, minced
1 egg
3 tablespoons flour
1½ quarts beef stock
4 eggs
4 tablespoons lemon juice

Mix together the ground meat, onion, parsley, rice, salt, garlic, and egg, and shape into small ¾-inch balls. Roll in flour. Heat beef stock to boiling in a large soup kettle, add meatballs, cover, and simmer 35 minutes, or until rice is tender. Beat the eggs and lemon juice until blended; pour in 1 cup of the hot broth, stirring briskly, then return mixture to the pan. Heat gently, without simmering, until thickened. Makes 6 servings.

It is festive to serve the platter of chicken, carrots, and leeks on the side, letting it follow a first course of lemon soup.

Chicken and Leek Soup / *Kota me Prasa Soupa*

> 1 broiler-fryer (about 3 pounds)
> 2 tablespoons chicken stock base
> Salt
> 1 onion, quartered
> 6 whole peppercorns
> 1 bay leaf
> 1 bunch carrots
> 1 bunch leeks
> 2 tablespoons cornstarch
> 2 tablespoons water
> 4 eggs
> ¼ cup lemon juice

Wash chicken well. Place in a soup kettle with 1½ quarts water, chicken stock base, salt to taste, onion, peppercorns, and bay leaf. Cover and simmer for 1¼ to 1½ hours, or until chicken is tender. Remove chicken from broth and set aside to cool slightly. Peel and trim carrots and cut lengthwise. Wash leeks well and halve lengthwise. Place carrots and leeks in broth and simmer 10 minutes, or until tender. Remove to an ovenproof platter. Remove the cooked chicken meat from the carcass, and arrange meat with vegetables on the platter; cover and keep warm in a 250° oven.

Strain broth and skim off fat. Cook down until reduced slightly and richly flavored (you should have about a quart). Spoon about ¼ cup broth over the chicken and vegetables.

Blend cornstarch with 2 tablespoons water. Bring broth to a boil, and blend in the cornstarch paste; boil 2 minutes. Beat eggs and lemon juice until blended. Pour half the broth into the eggs, whisk until blended, return to pan, and heat over very low heat, stirring, until thickened. Serve in a tureen with the chicken and vegetable platter alongside. Makes about 6 servings.

Traditional Greek families break the Lenten fast with this classic holiday soup, savored after the midnight service. The entrails of the lamb that is killed for spit roasting on Easter are basic to Mageritsa. *Because lamb's lung and intestines are hard to come by, they are omitted here, but if they are available, thoroughly wash 1 pound intestines and 1 pair lungs, parboil along with hearts, and chop finely with other meats.*

Easter Soup / *Mageritsa*

    2 lamb hearts
    1½ pounds lamb liver
    1 small onion, quartered
    1 stalk celery, cut up
    ½ cup lemon juice
    Salt and pepper
    ½ cup butter
    2 bunches green onions, finely chopped
    ½ cup finely chopped fresh parsley
    ¼ cup fresh chopped dill or 1 tablespoon dried
       dill
    Chicken stock
    ½ cup rice
    6 eggs
    2 tablespoons cornstarch

Wash meat parts well. Place hearts in a large saucepan with onion, celery, 3 tablespoons of the lemon juice, 1 pint water, and salt and pepper to taste. Bring to a boil, skim off scum, cover, and simmer 30 minutes; add livers and simmer 15 minutes longer. Strain, reserving broth. Finely chop meats.

Heat butter in a soup kettle and brown meats. Add green onions, parsley, and dill, and sauté a few minutes. Add reserved broth and enough chicken stock to make 2½ quarts. Bring to a boil, add rice, cover, and simmer 20 minutes. Beat eggs until blended, and beat in cornstarch stirred into remaining lemon juice. Slowly pour in 2 cups of the hot broth. Gradually pour mixture back into the soup and cook over low heat, stirring, until mixture coats a spoon. Makes 8 to 10 servings.

🔖

Skordalia sauce, shrieking with garlic, is an appealing accompaniment to dollop into this aromatic fish stew. For the fish buy halibut, sea bass, or striped bass.

Fish Soup / *Psarasoupa*

> 1 medium-sized onion, finely chopped
> 1 stalk celery, finely chopped
> ⅓ cup olive oil
> 1½ quarts water (or 1 quart water and 1 pint clam juice)
> 1 cup dry white wine or vermouth (optional)
> Salt and pepper
> 2½-pound piece firm white fish, tied in cheesecloth
> 12 small new potatoes, scrubbed and peeled
> 1 bunch leeks, trimmed and cut in half lengthwise
> ¼ cup lemon juice
> 2 tablespoons finely chopped fresh parsley

Using a large soup kettle, sauté onion and celery in 1 tablespoon of the oil until limp. Add water (or water and clam juice), wine, and salt and pepper to taste, and bring to a boil. Add fish in cheesecloth and the potatoes. Cover and simmer 10 minutes. Add leeks and simmer 10 minutes longer, or until fish is tender and flakes with a fork. Remove fish from broth and place on a platter; remove skin and bones. Spoon potatoes and leeks alongside. Mix remaining olive oil with lemon juice and parsley, spoon half of it over fish, and stir remainder into soup. Serve soup as a first course and follow with fish and vegetable platter. Serves 6.

AVGOLEMONO VARIATION. Omit the olive oil, lemon juice, and parsley sauce. Beat together until blended 4 eggs and ¼ cup lemon juice. Pour the hot prepared broth into the egg mixture, whisking constantly. Return to the pan and heat over low heat, stirring, until broth is thickened.

❧

Oven-browning the veal bones first lends richness to the finished broth. Beef shanks may replace the veal knuckle.

Veal Broth with Lemon / *Moskari Zoumos Avgolemono*

2-pound veal knuckle with some meat, cut in 2-inch pieces
Salt and pepper
1 medium-sized onion, finely chopped
1 bunch leeks, washed and sliced (use only part of the green tops)
2 tablespoons olive oil
4 eggs
¼ cup lemon juice

Sprinkle veal knuckle with salt and pepper and place in a roasting pan. Roast at 425° for 40 minutes or until well browned. Transfer to a soup kettle. Add 1½ quarts water, cover, and simmer for 2 hours, or until meat falls from the bones. Remove bones and meat from broth, and skim off fat. Dice the meat and return to broth.

Sauté onion and leeks in the oil until transparent, and add to the broth. Simmer for 10 minutes, or until vegetables are tender. Beat together the eggs and lemon juice until blended; pour in 1 cup of the hot broth, stirring briskly. Return mixture to the pan and heat gently, without simmering, until thickened. Makes 6 servings.

🦋

Orzo is a small, seed-shaped pasta traditionally used in soups and giouvetsi. *Look for it in a Near Eastern delicatessen.*

Beef Soup with Pasta / *Soupa Vothini me Rizi*

> 1½ pounds beef shank, cut in 2-inch pieces
> 2 tablespoons olive oil
> 1 onion, chopped
> 1 carrot, chopped
> Salt and pepper
> 1 can (15 ounces) whole peeled tomatoes
> ½ cup orzo or egg noodles

Using a large soup kettle, brown beef shank in oil. Add onion and carrot, and cook until glazed. Add 1½ quarts water, salt and pepper to taste, tomatoes and their juices, and bring to a boil. Cover and simmer for 2 hours, or until meat is tender. Remove bones and meat from broth, and skim off fat. Strain broth, pressing vegetables through a sieve. Bring to a boil, add orzo, and cook until tender, about 12 minutes. Remove meat from bones, cut in small pieces, and return to broth. Heat until hot through. Makes 6 to 8 servings.

🌺

The vinegar here is typically Greek. You may substitute wine for less piquancy.

Lentil Soup / *Faki Soupa*

1 medium-sized onion, finely chopped
1 stalk celery, finely chopped
1 carrot, chopped (optional)
3 tablespoons olive oil
1½ cups quick-cooking lentils
1 bay leaf
1 clove garlic, minced
½ teaspoon salt
Freshly ground pepper
3 tablespoons tomato paste
¼ cup red wine vinegar or dry red wine
½ teaspoon oregano

Using a soup kettle, sauté onion, celery, and carrot in oil until limp. Add the lentils, bay leaf, garlic, salt, pepper, and 2 quarts water. Cover and simmer until tender, according to package directions. Add the tomato paste, vinegar or wine, and oregano, and simmer 30 minutes longer. Serves 8.

This is a hearty soup, especially popular during Lent. In the villages it is typical Friday fare with pickled vegetables and chopped raw onion.

Bean Soup / *Fassoulada Soupa*

1½ cups small white dried beans, Great Northern
beans, or baby lima beans
1 large onion, finely chopped
2 carrots, finely chopped
1 stalk celery, chopped
2 cloves garlic, minced
¼ cup olive oil
1 bay leaf
2 tablespoons beef stock base
1 can (8 ounces) tomato sauce
Salt and pepper
Finely chopped parsley

Cover beans with water and bring to a boil. Cook 2 minutes, cover, and let stand 1 hour; drain. In a large soup kettle, sauté onion, carrots, celery, and garlic in oil until vegetables are limp. Add beans, 2 quarts water, bay leaf, and beef stock base, and bring to a boil. Cover and simmer until beans are tender, about 45 minutes. Add tomato sauce and salt and pepper to taste. Cover and simmer 10 minutes longer. If necessary, add more water to thin to desired consistency. Sprinkle with parsley. Makes 6 to 8 servings.

This is a wonderfully refreshing icy summer soup. Ground walnuts are a surprise. Buttermilk may replace the yogurt and milk.

Yogurt Soup / *Yiaourti Soupa*

⅓ cup shelled walnuts
2 cloves garlic, peeled
¼ cup olive oil
2 tablespoons white wine vinegar
3 cups yogurt
1 cup milk
1 cucumber, peeled and finely chopped
Salt and pepper
Finely chopped parsley

In a blender container place the walnuts, garlic, oil, and vinegar, and blend until smooth. (Or mash with a mortar and pestle.) Empty into a mixing bowl, and stir in the yogurt and milk, stirring until smooth. Add the cucumber and salt and pepper to taste. Sprinkle with parsley. Serve cold. Makes 6 servings.

SALADS

Throughout the mainland and the isles this cheese-dressed salad appears with infinite local variation. Fresh herbs are often added with abandon and the greens omitted. It is also called Greek salad or rural salad.

Country Salad / *Salata Horiatiki*

- 1 head chicory (curly endive)
- 1 head iceberg lettuce
- 2 cucumbers, peeled and sliced
- 2 tomatoes, cut in wedges, or 1 cup cherry tomatoes, halved
- 2 dozen Greek olives
- 2 green onions, chopped
- 2 tablespoons large capers (optional)
- ½ cup olive oil
- 3 tablespoons red wine vinegar
- ½ teaspoon salt
- ½ teaspoon dried oregano
- Freshly ground pepper
- 8 anchovy fillets
- ¼ pound feta cheese, crumbled

Tear the chicory and lettuce into bite-size pieces and place in a large salad bowl. Add the cucumbers, tomatoes, olives, onions, and capers. Shake together the oil, vinegar, salt, oregano, and pepper and pour over salad. Mix well. Garnish with anchovy fillets, chopped if desired, and sprinkle with cheese. Makes 8 servings.

This mixed vegetable salad enhances lamb or fish. It also can serve as an appetizer to spread on lavosh *or sesame crackers.*

Eggplant Salad / *Melitzanes Salata*

1 large eggplant
1 medium-sized onion, grated, or 4 green onions, finely chopped
1 large tomato, peeled and chopped
1 clove garlic, minced
2 tablespoons chopped parsley
½ teaspoon dried marjoram
⅓ cup olive oil
2 tablespoons red wine vinegar
½ teaspoon salt
Freshly ground pepper
Romaine leaves
Chopped parsley
Greek olives

Place the whole eggplant in a shallow pan and bake in a 350° oven for 1 hour. Dip into cold water and peel off the skin. Dice the eggplant into small pieces and place in a bowl. Add the onion, tomato, garlic, parsley, marjoram, oil, vinegar, salt, and pepper. Mix well and chill several hours for flavors to blend. Serve mounds of salad in Romaine leaves, sprinkle with parsley, and garnish with olives. Makes 6 servings.

🦂

This cool salad complements fish or seafood.

Cucumbers with Yogurt / *Angourosalata me Yiaourti*

3 medium-sized cucumbers
2 cloves garlic, minced
3 green onions, finely chopped
1 tablespoon fresh chopped dill, or ¾ teaspoon dried dill
Salt and freshly ground pepper
1 tablespoon white wine vinegar
1 cup (½ pint) yogurt
Finely chopped parsley

Peel cucumbers; slice thinly or grate on the slicer side of the grater. Place in a bowl, and add garlic, onions, dill, and salt and pepper to taste. Mix together the vinegar and yogurt and add to the salad, mixing well. Garnish with parsley. Makes 6 servings.

🦂

The flavor-packed big beefsteak tomatoes and fresh garden herbs are excellent here.

Sliced Tomatoes with Feta / *Domatosalata me Feta*

⅓ cup olive oil
2 tablespoons white wine vinegar
1 clove garlic, minced
1 tablespoon chopped fresh herbs (basil, oregano, marjoram, tarragon), or ¾ teaspoon dried basil
1 teaspoon Worcestershire sauce
Salt and pepper
½ cup crumbled feta cheese
4 beefsteak tomatoes
2 dozen Greek olives

For dressing, place in a jar the oil, vinegar, garlic, herbs, Worcestershire, salt and pepper to taste, and cheese; cover and shake well. Chill until ready to use. Peel and slice tomatoes, and arrange on a platter. Scatter olives over tomatoes. Shake dressing well and pour over. Makes 6 to 8 servings.

A sophisticated Greek restaurant, the White Tower in London, serves this handsome fish first course. Consider it for a summer dinner entrée as well.

Aegean Fish Salad / *Psari Salata me Avgolemono*

2 pounds sliced halibut or swordfish steaks
1½ cups water
1 bay leaf

4 whole black peppercorns
1 small onion, peeled and quartered
3 slices lemon
1 teaspoon salt
1 cucumber
1½ cups cherry tomatoes
Avgolemono dressing (see below)
1 dozen medium shrimp, cooked, peeled, and
  deveined
Greek olives

Place fish steaks in a single layer in a large frying pan (with a cover). Add the water, bay leaf, peppercorns, onion, lemon, and salt. Cover and simmer for 8 minutes, or until fish is tender. Let cool, and drain off stock, reserving it for dressing. Chill fish.

To serve, arrange fish steaks in a row on a large platter. Thinly slice unpeeled cucumber and arrange along one side. Halve tomatoes and arrange on the other side. Spoon dressing over the fish, and garnish with shrimp and olives. Makes 6 servings.

AVGOLEMONO DRESSING. Strain fish stock and cook down until reduced to ½ cup. Beat 2 egg yolks and 1 tablespoon lemon juice until blended. Pour the hot fish stock into the egg yolk mixture, beating until blended. Pour into the top of a double boiler and place over hot water, stirring, until sauce is thickened. Let cool. Stir in ½ cup sour cream and chill until ready to use.

Coral tarama heaped in avocado half-shells makes an eye-catching still life. It is a superb prelude to chicken or fish.

Avocado with *Taramosalata* / *Avocado me Taramosalata*

3 medium-sized avocados
2 tablespoons lemon juice
Chicory, Boston or Australian lettuce
1 cup *taramosalata* (see page 17)
1 lemon
Watercress (optional)

Leave avocados unpeeled; halve and remove seeds. Sprinkle cut surface with lemon juice. Place each avocado half on a bed of greens on a salad plate. Mound *taramosalata* in each half. Cut lemon into 6 wedges and garnish each salad with a lemon wedge and a few sprigs of watercress. Serves 6.

This striking seafood salad is also excellent with crab meat and mushrooms replacing the shrimp and tomatoes.

Artichoke, Shrimp, and Tomato Salad / *Anginarokardoules, me Garides, me Domato Salata*

3 jars (6 ounces *each*) marinated artichoke hearts
⅓ cup lemon juice
½ teaspoon dried tarragon or basil
1 clove garlic, minced
Salt and freshly ground pepper
1 head chicory, Boston, or Australian lettuce
1½ pounds cooked medium shrimp, peeled and deveined
3 cups cherry tomatoes, halved

Drain the marinade from the artichoke hearts into a bowl and add to it the lemon juice, tarragon or basil, garlic, and salt and pepper to taste; stir to blend. Line a large shallow salad bowl with greens, and arrange artichoke hearts in a row on one side. Place shrimp in a row down the center and arrange halved tomatoes on the other side. Spoon the dressing over. Makes 10 to 12 servings.

ARTICHOKE, CRAB, AND MUSHROOM SALAD. Follow above recipe, but omit shrimp and tomatoes. Substitute 2 cans (7¾ ounces *each*) Dungeness or Alaska King crab meat and ¾ pound raw mushrooms. Slice mushrooms, if large; otherwise leave whole and marinate in half the dressing for 15 minutes before arranging salad.

Cold sliced meats and hard-cooked eggs may accompany this hot vegetable salad for lunch or supper.

Hot Potato Salad / *Zesti Patatosalata*

> 6 medium-sized potatoes
> 1 bunch green onions, finely chopped
> ½ cup olive oil
> 3 tablespoons white wine vinegar or lemon juice
> Salt and pepper
> 1 teaspoon dried dill or oregano
> Finely chopped parsley

Cook unpeeled potatoes in boiling salted water until tender, about 20 minutes; drain and rinse under cold water. Peel and slice into a salad bowl. Add onions. Shake together the oil, vinegar or lemon juice, salt and pepper to taste, and dill or oregano, and pour over potatoes. Mix lightly. Sprinkle with parsley. Makes 6 to 8 servings.

🦎

For a delightful surprise, cinnamon spices the lemon dressing of this fresh spinach salad, strewn with salty cheese. Ribbons of feta, eggs, and cucumber adorn the top. This is a green salad that holds up well on a buffet table.

Spinach and Feta Salad / *Spanako me Feta Salata*

2 pounds (approximately) fresh spinach
½ cup olive oil
2 tablespoons white wine vinegar
2 tablespoons lemon juice
¼ teaspoon cinnamon
¼ teaspoon dry mustard
½ teaspoon salt
Freshly ground pepper
2 cucumbers
4 hard-cooked eggs
¼ pound feta cheese, crumbled
2 green onions, chopped

Remove stems from spinach. Wash and drain leaves, cut into 1-inch-wide strips, and place in a salad bowl. Shake together the oil, vinegar, lemon juice, cinnamon, mustard, salt, and pepper; pour half the dressing over the spinach and mix well. Thinly slice cucumbers (leave peel on, if you wish), and arrange in a row across the top. Slice eggs and arrange alongside. Sprinkle the cheese and onions over all. Pour remaining dressing over salad. Makes 8 servings.

VEGETABLES

For a choice luncheon or supper dish, consider artichoke shells filled with a creamy ham and cheese sauce. Assemble in advance and chill, if you wish; then bake just before serving.

Artichokes Béchamel / *Anginares Besamel*

8 large artichokes
Lemon juice
1 cup finely chopped cooked ham or Canadian bacon
2 cups béchamel sauce (see page 129)
⅓ pound feta cheese, crumbled
1 cup freshly shredded Parmesan cheese
¼ cup fine dry bread crumbs or crushed zwieback
3 tablespoons melted butter

Cut the stems from artichokes so they will stand upright. Peel off the tough outer leaves and, with kitchen scissors, cut the tips off all remaining leaves. Rub the cut portions with lemon. Cook in boiling salted water until tender, but not soft, about 35 to 40 minutes. Drain well and scoop out the center choke with a spoon. Place upright in a lightly buttered baking dish.

Mix together the ham or bacon, béchamel sauce, feta cheese, and half the Parmesan cheese. Spoon some of the mixture inside each artichoke. Sprinkle with crumbs and remaining Parmesan cheese, and drizzle with butter. Bake in a 350° oven for 20 minutes or until the cheese topping browns lightly. Makes 8 servings.

CASSEROLE VARIATION. Cook 2 packages (8 ounces *each*) artichoke hearts in boiling salted water for 5 to 7 minutes, or until tender; drain. Arrange on a buttered baking dish. Spoon the sauce, crumbs, cheese, and melted butter over artichoke hearts. Bake as directed above.

🦋

Freshly grated Kasseri—a firm, sharp goat cheese—lends zest to asparagus.

Asparagus with Kasseri / *Sparagia me Kasseri*

2 pounds fresh asparagus
⅓ cup butter
½ cup shredded Kasseri or Romano cheese

Wash asparagus and snap off tough ends; trim. Cook in boiling salted water just until barely tender, about 7 minutes; drain. Turn out on a serving platter and keep warm. Heat butter until it sizzles and starts to turn brown; pour over asparagus and sprinkle with cheese. Makes 6 servings.

🦋

Fresh dill enhances this colorful vegetable arrangement, punctuated by a sprightly oil and lemon sauce that also permeates the vegetables as they simmer. If the tiny artichokes (about 1 to 1½ inches in diameter) aren't available, substitute 4 small artichokes (about 3 to 4 inches in diameter).

Artichokes à la Constantinople / *Anginares a la Polita*

    16 tiny baby artichokes
    ¼ cup lemon juice
    2 tablespoons flour
    8 small carrots, peeled and cut in 1½-inch
       lengths
    2 potatoes, peeled and diced in 1-inch pieces
    2 bunches green onions, cut in 1½-inch lengths
    1 cup olive oil
    ½ cup lemon juice
    Salt and pepper
    1 tablespoon chopped fresh dill, or 1½ teaspoons
       dried dill

Peel off the outer leaves of artichokes, discarding all the tough leaves; cut in half lengthwise, and scrape out the chokes with a spoon. Let soak in salted cold water to cover with ¼ cup lemon juice and the flour to prevent artichokes from turning dark while preparing the other ingredients.

In a Dutch oven or large frying pan place the drained, trimmed artichokes, carrots, potatoes, onions, oil, lemon juice, 1 cup water, salt and pepper to taste, and dill. Cover and simmer for 25 minutes, or until artichokes are tender. If necessary, remove cover and cook down juices so sauce is very thick. Transfer to a serving platter and spoon sauce over vegetables. Makes 8 servings.

🌺

Meat-stuffed artichokes make a handsome, easy-to-serve hot luncheon entrée.

Stuffed Artichokes / *Anginares Yemistes*

> 8 large artichokes
> Lemon juice
> 1 pound ground pork or beef
> 1 large onion, finely chopped
> 5 tablespoons butter
> ½ cup dry red wine
> 1 can (8 ounces) tomato sauce
> 1 clove garlic, minced
> 1 tablespoon chopped parsley
> 1 teaspoon salt
> Pepper
> 1 cup béchamel sauce (see page 129)
> ¼ cup fine dry bread crumbs or crushed zwieback
> ½ cup shredded Romano cheese

Cut the stems from artichokes so they will stand upright. Peel off the tough outer leaves and, with kitchen scissors, cut the tips off all remaining leaves. Rub the cut portions with lemon. Cook in boiling salted water until tender, but not soft, about 35 to 40 minutes. Drain well and scoop out the center choke with a spoon. Place upright in a lightly buttered baking dish.

Meanwhile, in a large frying pan brown the meat and onion in 2 tablespoons of the butter, stirring until crumbly. Add wine, tomato sauce, garlic, parsley, salt, and pepper to taste. Cover and simmer 30 minutes, or until liquid is absorbed. Spoon meat mixture into the artichokes, spoon béchamel sauce over fillings, and sprinkle with crumbs and cheese. Melt remaining butter and drizzle over. Bake in a 350° oven for 20 minutes or until hot through and lightly browned. Serves 8.

A *lemon and herb vinaigrette sauce refreshes a whole steamed cauliflower.*

Cauliflower Oregano / *Kounoupidi Riganati*

    1 large cauliflower
    3 tablespoons olive oil
    3 tablespoons lemon juice
    1 tablespoon minced parsley
    ½ teaspoon dried oregano
    ¼ teaspoon salt

Trim cauliflower and cook whole in boiling salted water for 15 minutes, or until barely tender; drain and place on a serving platter. Meanwhile, mix together the oil, lemon juice, parsley, oregano, and salt. Pour dressing over cauliflower. Serves 6.

ARTICHOKE VARIATION. Peel outer leaves, halve, and core 2 dozen tiny baby artichokes (drop into cold water with 2 teaspoons salt and 2 tablespoons lemon juice as you do this). Drain and cook in boiling salted water with 3 tablespoons lemon juice for 15 minutes, or until tender; drain. (Or substitute 2 8-ounce packages frozen artichoke hearts. Cook in boiling salted water 5 to 7 minutes; drain.) Place on a serving dish and spoon over the lemon-oil dressing. Serves 6.

BROCCOLI VARIATION. Trim stalks from 1 large bunch broccoli. Cook flowerets in boiling salted water until tender, about 8 to 10 minutes; drain and place on a serving platter. Add 1 clove minced garlic to the lemon-oil sauce and spoon over. Serves 6.

🦂

A succulent lamb and vegetable mélange bakes inside a whole regal eggplant.

Stuffed Eggplant / *Melitzanes Yemistes*

    2   medium-sized onions, finely chopped
    1   pound ground lamb or veal
    ⅓ cup olive oil
    1   carrot, finely chopped
    1   stalk celery, chopped
    ⅓ cup parsley, chopped
    2   tomatoes, peeled and chopped
    2   cloves garlic, minced
  1½ teaspoons salt
      Freshly ground pepper
    2   teaspoons chopped fresh basil or oregano,
       or ½ teaspoon dried basil
    1   large eggplant
    2   tablespoons long-grain white rice
    ¾ cup water

Sauté onions and ground meat in oil until meat is browned, stirring until crumbly. Add carrot, celery, parsley, tomatoes, garlic, salt, pepper, and basil or oregano. Cover and simmer until tender, about 25 minutes. Slice off the stem end of the eggplant to make a lid, and with a spoon scoop out the pulp, leaving a shell about 1 inch thick. Sprinkle the inside lightly with salt. Chop the scooped-out eggplant pulp into cubes and add to the vegetables; simmer 15 minutes longer. Stir in rice. Rinse out the salted eggplant, drain well, and spoon in the vegetable mixture. Replace eggplant lid and secure with toothpicks. Place in a deep casserole and pour in ¾ cup water. Cover and bake in a 350° oven for 1 hour. Cut in slices to serve. Makes 6 to 8 servings.

Lemon sauce smothers these meat-filled leaves to serve as a first course, entrée, or side dish with roast lamb or chicken.

Meat-Stuffed Grape or Cabbage Leaves / *Dolmathes*

1 pound ground lamb or beef
1 large onion, finely chopped
1 tablespoon olive oil
2 leaves fresh mint, chopped
1 clove garlic, minced
1 small tomato, peeled and chopped
¾ teaspoon salt
¼ teaspoon pepper
½ cup water
3 tablespoons long-grain white rice
1 jar grape leaves (about 3 to 4 dozen) or fresh
   grape leaves or 2 small green cabbages

1½ cups beef broth
2 tablespoons butter, melted
1 egg
2 egg yolks
3 tablespoons lemon juice

Using a large frying pan, brown meat and onion in oil. Add mint, garlic, tomato, salt, pepper, and ½ cup water; cover and simmer 30 minutes. Mix in the rice and remove from heat.

Remove grape leaves from the jar, scald with hot water, and drain. Or blanch fresh grape leaves or cabbage leaves (about 4 inches in diameter) in boiling salted water for 1 minute; lift out with a slotted spoon and drain.

Place about 1 tablespoon filling at the stem end of grape or cabbage leaves, fold sides in, and roll up. Arrange in a large frying pan, seam side down. Pour the broth and melted butter over. Cover and simmer 50 minutes to 1 hour, or until rice is tender.

For lemon sauce, beat together the egg, egg yolks, and lemon juice. Pour the broth from the stuffed leaves into the lemon-egg mixture and beat just until blended. Return to the pan and cook over very low heat just until the sauce is thickened. Makes about 3 dozen stuffed leaves: 6 to 8 first-course servings or 4 entrée servings.

The Greeks prize such slightly bitter greens as dandelion, mustard, kale, escarole, chicory, spinach, and Swiss chard, and cultivate them in the garden. They are favored especially with fish.

Greens Sauté / *Horta Tighanita*

> 1½ pounds greens (see above)
> 2 cloves garlic, minced
> 3 tablespoons olive oil
> ½ teaspoon dried oregano
> 1 lemon, cut in wedges

Wash greens thoroughly and trim off coarse stems. Parboil in a small amount of boiling salted water for 2 or 3 minutes or longer, depending on the greens; drain well. Using a large frying pan, sauté garlic in oil; add drained greens and oregano, and cook 5 to 10 minutes longer, shaking pan, until greens are tender. Garnish with lemon wedges. Serves 4.

An herb-seasoned vegetable sauce gilds green beans as they braise.

Braised Green Beans / *Fassoulakia Yahni*

> 1 bunch green onions, finely chopped
> 3 tablespoons olive oil
> 1½ pounds green beans
> 2 tomatoes, peeled and chopped
> 1 clove garlic, minced
> ¼ cup finely chopped parsley
> Salt and pepper

Using a heavy saucepan, sauté onions in oil until glazed. Cut off the tips of the green beans and slice in half lengthwise; add to the onions along with tomatoes, garlic, parsley, and salt and pepper to taste. Cover and simmer for 20 minutes, or until tender. Serves 6.

🦎

Here freshly shredded pumpkin or winter squash, enhanced with nuts and honey, bakes between fila layers for a versatile vegetable side dish or dessert.

Pumpkin or Squash Pita / *Kolokethopita*

6 cups shredded fresh pumpkin or banana squash
1 cup sugar
1 cup finely chopped walnuts
½ cup golden raisins
1 cup crushed wheat cereal or corn cereal flakes
1 teaspoon salt
1 teaspoon cinnamon
3 tablespoons honey
½ cup butter, melted
12 sheets prepared fila dough

Mix together lightly the pumpkin or squash, sugar, nuts, raisins, cereal flakes, salt, cinnamon, honey, and 2 tablespoons of the butter.

Lay out fila and cover with clear plastic film to keep from drying out. Line a buttered 9-by-13-inch baking pan with one sheet of fila, brush with melted butter, and cover with 5 more sheets of fila, brushing each with melted butter and letting fila overlap the sides of the pan. Spoon pumpkin or squash mixture into the fila-lined pan and smooth top. Fold any overhanging fila back over the filling. Arrange 6 more buttered sheets of fila, cut or folded in to fit top of the pan, one at a time on top.

Using a razor blade or sharp knife, cut squares through the top layers of fila only, making 3 lengthwise and 5 crosswise cuts, or cut diagonally into diamonds. Bake in a 375° oven for 1 hour, or until filling is tender when pierced with a knife. Remove to a rack and finish cutting into squares. Serve warm or chilled. Makes 24 pieces.

🦎

Green rice, streaked with spinach and leeks, provides an apropos side dish to fish or lamb.

Spinach and Rice / *Spanakonzo*

      1 medium-sized onion, finely chopped
      1 bunch leeks, washed and chopped, or 2
          bunches green onions, chopped
      6 tablespoons olive oil
      ¾ cup long-grain rice
      1 clove garlic, minced
      2 pounds fresh spinach, washed and chopped
      1½ cups chicken or beef broth
      1 teaspoon salt
          Freshly ground pepper
          Lemon wedges (optional)

In a Dutch oven or flameproof casserole, sauté onion and leeks in oil until limp. Add rice, garlic, spinach, broth, salt, and pepper; cover and simmer for 20 minutes, or until rice is tender. Serve hot with lemon wedges, if desired. Makes 6 servings.

These vegetable pastry squares, filled with greens and feta, are excellent served warm, tepid, or chilled. They particularly complement roast lamb and are an integral part of the Easter dinner menu.

Spinach Pie / *Spanakopita*

> 2 pounds (approximately) fresh spinach
> 1 bunch chicory (curly endive)
> 1 bunch parsley
> 1 bunch green onions
> 6 leaves fresh mint
> 1 tablespoon salt
> Freshly ground pepper
> ¼ cup olive oil
> 4 eggs, slightly beaten
> ¼ cup fine dry bread crumbs
> ¾ pound feta, crumbled
> Dash of nutmeg
> 12 sheets prepared fila dough
> 6 tablespoons butter, melted

Wash greens and pat dry thoroughly. Finely chop the spinach, chicory, parsley, onions, and mint, and pat dry again. Place in a large bowl and mix in the salt, pepper, oil, eggs, crumbs, feta, and nutmeg.

Lay out fila and cover with clear plastic film to keep from drying out. Line a buttered 9-by-13-inch baking pan with one sheet of fila, brush with melted butter, and cover with 5 more sheets of fila, brushing each with melted butter and letting fila overlap sides of the pan. Place the greens mix-

ture in the fila-lined pan and smooth the top. Fold any overhanging fila back over the greens. Arrange 6 more buttered
sheets of fila, cut or folded in to fit top of the pan, one at a
time on top.

Using a razor blade or sharp knife, cut squares through
the top layers of fila only, making 3 lengthwise and 5 crosswise cuts. Bake in a 375° oven for 1 hour, or until greens
are tender. Remove to a rack and finish cutting into squares.
Serve warm, at room temperature, or chilled. Makes 24
pieces.

🌺

*Key seasonings provide an aromatic sauce for braising
squash.*

Steamed Summer Squash / *Kolokithia Vrasta*

   2 pounds zucchini or yellow crookneck squash
      (or a mixture of both), sliced
   1 medium-sized onion, finely chopped
   1 tomato, peeled and chopped
   2 cloves garlic, minced
   4 teaspoon dried oregano
   Salt and pepper
   2 cup olive oil

Place the sliced squash in a saucepan and add the onion, tomato, garlic, oregano, salt and pepper to taste, and
oil. Cover and simmer for 15 minutes, or until vegetables
are barely tender. Remove cover and cook down rapidly to
evaporate juices. Serves 6 to 8.

🌺

A beef and pine nut stuffing fills plump tomatoes, and a lemon sauce coats them all. Scooped-out zucchini or red or green peppers make neat containers also.

Stuffed Tomatoes / *Yemistes Domates Avgolemono*

    12 medium-sized tomatoes
    1 bunch green onions, finely chopped (use only
        part of green stems)
    2 tablespoons olive oil
    ½ cup finely chopped parsley
    3 tablespoons short-grain rice
    1 pound lean ground beef
    ½ teaspoon salt
    ⅓ cup pine nuts
    2 cups beef stock
    Avgolemono sauce (see below)

Slice the tops off the tomatoes, and use a spoon to scoop out the pulp, leaving a shell about ¾ inch thick. Finely chop the pulp and reserve, along with the juice. Using a large enamel frying pan, sauté onions in oil until limp; add parsley, rice, the reserved tomato pulp, meat, and salt; cover and simmer for 20 minutes, stirring occasionally. Mix in pine nuts, and if necessary, cook down until juices are evaporated. Spoon into the hollowed-out tomatoes.

Arrange stuffed tomatoes in the frying pan, pour in the beef stock, cover, and simmer for 4 minutes, or until tomatoes are barely tender. Transfer to a serving platter and keep warm; reserve stock. Serve surrounded with *avgolemono* sauce, and pass remaining sauce to pour over. Serves 6.

AVGOLEMONO SAUCE. Measure the reserved beef stock and cook down or add water to make 2 cups; heat to boiling. Beat 2 eggs until light, and blend in 2 tablespoons lemon juice. Pour in the hot stock, stirring constantly; return to pan and place over very low heat, stirring occasionally, until thickened.

ZUCCHINI VARIATION. Instead of tomatoes, substitute 12 large zucchini squash, about 1½ inches in diameter. Trim the ends from the squash, then cut squash in 2-inch lengths, and use an apple corer to hollow out the insides of the squash, leaving a shell ⅓ inch thick. Proceed as for stuffed tomatoes above, substituting 1 large tomato, peeled and chopped, for the hollowed-out tomato pulp in the meat stuffing. Simmer stuffed squash for 8 to 10 minutes, or until barely tender. Serves 6.

PEPPER VARIATION. Substitute 12 medium-sized green or red bell peppers for the tomatoes in the recipe above. Slice the tops from the peppers and discard the seeds. Proceed as in basic recipe, substituting 1 large tomato, peeled and chopped, for the hollowed-out tomato pulp in the meat stuffing. Simmer stuffed peppers for 8 to 10 minutes, or until barely tender. Serves 6.

Either one or several vegetables may poach in succession in this aromatic herb bath. The cooking liquid is reduced to a thick sauce to dress the vegetables, and the dish is served hot, tepid, or chilled.

Vegetables Greek Style / *Vegetables à la Grecque*

2½ cups water
¼ cup dry vermouth or white wine
3 tablespoons lemon juice
¼ cup olive oil
1 green onion, chopped
Few peppercorns
1 teaspoon salt
¼ teaspoon dried thyme
3 sprigs parsley
Vegetables: 2 pounds mushrooms or an assortment: carrots, leeks, zucchini, crookneck squash, eggplant
Minced parsley

In a large enamel saucepan or Dutch oven combine the water, the wine, lemon juice, oil, onion, peppercorns, salt, thyme, and parsley sprigs. Cover and simmer 10 minutes for seasonings to blend. Add prepared vegetables as suggested below, and simmer as directed. Remove vegetables with a slotted spoon to a serving dish.

Rapidly boil down juices until reduced to about ⅔ cup. Spoon over the vegetables. Serve hot, or let cool to room temperature, or cover and chill. Sprinkle with minced parsley. Serves 8.

For mushrooms, trim and wash. Leave whole if small or halve if large. Add to broth and simmer 5 minutes.

For carrots, peel and cut lengthwise. Add to broth and simmer 10 minutes, or until crisp tender.

For leeks, trim ends, cut lengthwise, and wash thoroughly. Add to broth and simmer 15 to 20 minutes, or until tender.

For zucchini and crookneck squash, trim ends and halve lengthwise. Add to broth and simmer 8 to 10 minutes, or until crisp tender.

For eggplant, cut in lengthwise wedges and leave peel on, if desired. Add to broth and simmer 8 to 10 minutes, or until tender.

🔖

A mélange of half a dozen vegetables bakes together for a marvelous intermingling and fusion of flavors.

Vegetable Oven Stew / Lahana Tou Fournou

> 1 medium-sized onion, finely chopped
> ¼ cup olive oil
> 6 small zucchini squash, sliced
> ½ pound green beans, cut in 2-inch pieces
> 2 medium-sized carrots, sliced
> 2 medium-sized potatoes, cut in lengthwise strips
> 2 stalks celery, cut in l-inch pieces
> 3 leaves fresh mint, chopped
> 2 cloves garlic, minced
> Salt and pepper
> 1 can (8 ounces) tomato sauce

Using a heavy flameproof casserole, sauté onion in oil until limp. Add the squash, beans, carrots, potatoes, celery, mint, garlic, salt and pepper to taste, and tomato sauce. Mix lightly. Cover and bake in a 325° oven for 1 hour, or until vegetables are tender. Serves 6 to 8.

RICE, PASTA, AND CHEESE DISHES

The Greek pilaf is made with long-grain rice. Vary the stock to suit the entrée it will accompany. For example, use chicken stock for poultry entrées, clam broth for seafood entrées, and beef stock for meats. The pan juices acquired in cooking the meat may substitute for part of the stock.

Rice Pilaf / *Pilafi*

    2 cups stock or water
    1 cup long-grain white rice
    2 tablespoons butter
    Salt

Bring stock to boiling, and add rice, butter, and salt (amount depending on seasonings in stock). Cover and simmer 20 minutes, or until liquid is absorbed. Makes 4 to 6 servings.

Herb-flavored pilaf, strewn with mushrooms, makes a grand accompaniment to roast chicken or lamb or barbecued chops or steaks.

Rice Pilaf with Mushrooms / *Pilafi me Manitaria*

> 1 medium-sized onion, finely chopped
> ½ cup butter
> 2 cloves garlic, minced
> 3 tablespoons finely chopped parsley
> ¼ teaspoon dried marjoram
> ¼ teaspoon dried thyme
> 1 cup long-grain white rice
> 1½ cups chicken or beef broth
> ½ cup dry white wine
> 1 pound mushrooms
> 2 tablespoons lemon juice
> ½ cup freshly grated Parmesan cheese

Using a heavy saucepan or flameproof casserole, sauté onion in ¼ cup of the butter. Add half the minced garlic, the parsley, marjoram, thyme, and rice, and sauté 1 minute, stirring until coated. Bring broth and wine to a boil, pour over rice, cover, and simmer for 20 minutes. Meanwhile, wash and trim mushrooms; leave whole if small or slice if large. Melt remaining butter with remaining garlic in a large frying pan. Add mushrooms and lemon juice and sauté quickly, 2 or 3 minutes, just until hot through and glazed. Add to the cooked rice, fluff with a fork, and sprinkle with cheese. Makes 6 servings.

A *popular pilaf is made by combining rice with a butter-browned crushed fine pasta, such as fide. Coiled capellinie or vermicelli may substitute.*

Rice and Pasta Pilaf / *Pilafi me Fides*

> ½ cup crushed fides or coiled capellinie or vermicelli
> ¼ cup butter
> 1 cup long-grain white rice
> 2½ cups hot chicken broth
> Salt and pepper
> Freshly grated Parmesan or Romano cheese (optional)

Using a large frying pan, sauté pasta in melted butter, stirring, until pasta turns golden brown. Add rice and stir until glazed. Pour in broth, add salt and pepper to taste, and cover and simmer for 20 minutes. If desired, sprinkle with cheese, fluff with a fork, cover, and let stand 5 to 10 minutes. Makes 4 to 6 servings.

This custardlike macaroni dish cuts cleanly into squares for easy serving at a large buffet party. Serve it hot or cooled to room temperature.

Macaroni Squares / *Pastitsio*

> 2 large onions, finely chopped
> ½ cup butter
> 2½ pounds lean ground beef

2 cans (8 ounces *each*) tomato sauce
2 teaspoons salt
2 cloves garlic, minced
1 stick cinnamon
1 package (14 ounces) large elbow macaroni
½ pound grated Romano cheese
Cinnamon
Custard sauce (see below)

Using a large frying pan, sauté onions in butter until golden. Add meat and cook until browned and crumbly. Add tomato sauce, salt, garlic, and cinnamon stick; cover and simmer for 30 minutes, or until thickened. Remove cinnamon stick.

Cook macaroni in a large amount of boiling salted water until barely tender, about 12 minutes; drain and rinse under cold water, then drain thoroughly. In a buttered 9-by-13-inch baking pan, alternate layers of macaroni, meat sauce, and cheese. Dust lightly with cinnamon. Pour custard sauce over macaroni, and finish off with a sprinkling of cheese. Bake in a 350° oven for 45 minutes, or until custard is set. Let cool slightly, then cut into squares. Makes 12 squares.

CUSTARD SAUCE.. Melt ¼ cup butter and blend in ¼ cup flour; gradually stir in 3 cups milk; stirring, cook until thickened. Add ½ teaspoon salt, ⅛ teaspoon nutmeg, and ⅛ teaspoon pepper. Beat 6 eggs until light and stir the hot sauce into the eggs.

Homemade egg noodles are easy but admittedly time-consuming to make. Their velvety texture and fresh flavor merit the effort.

Homemade Noodles / *Spitisies Hilopites*

> 1 egg
> 3 egg yolks
> 1 teaspoon olive oil
> ½ teaspoon salt
> 1½ cups unsifted all-purpose flour

Beat together just until blended the egg, egg yolks, oil, and salt. Spoon flour into a large mixing bowl and make a cavity in the center. Pour in the egg mixture and stir with a fork until flour is well moistened. Pat into a ball. Turn out on a lightly floured board and knead until dough is smooth and satiny, about 10 minutes.

Cut dough into 3 portions. Roll out 1 portion at a time until about 1/16 inch thick (keep the other sections covered with a towel so dough does not dry out). Transfer to lightly floured sheets of waxed paper and let sit uncovered while you roll the remaining dough. Roll up dough like a jelly roll and cut into strips of desired width. Unroll each strip and place on a towel to dry. If desired, cook at once in a large amount of boiling salted water for 5 minutes. Drain through a colander and rinse under a stream of cold water, shaking well. Use as instructed in recipe. Makes about 12 ounces.

This garlicky meat sauce achieves its captivating smoothness after long slow cooking. Mixed pickling spice is an amazing ingredient here. It is smart to make the sauce in quantity and freeze it. Then it is readily available for uses other than a pasta coating. It can go into pastitsio *or* moussaka, *fill avocado half-shells, or nestle in ramekins alongside artichoke hearts, sautéed mushrooms, or Italian green beans.*

Spaghetti with Meat Sauce / *Spageto me Kema*

    4 large onions, finely chopped
    ½ cup butter
    4 pounds lean ground beef
    2 teaspoons whole mixed pickling spice
    6 cloves garlic, minced
    4 cans (6 ounces *each*) tomato paste
    4 teaspoons salt
    Freshly ground pepper
    2 tablespoons red wine vinegar
    2 cups water
    Spaghetti
    Freshly grated Parmesan cheese

In a large Dutch oven, sauté onions in half the butter until golden brown. Remove from pan and set aside. Brown meat in remaining butter, stirring until crumbly, and return onions to pan. Tie spices in a cheesecloth bag or place in a tea ball, and add to pan with garlic, tomato paste, salt, pepper, vinegar, and water. Cover the pan and simmer, stirring occasionally, for 3 hours, or until sauce is thickened. Remove spices. If desired, let cool, ladle part of the sauce into freezer containers, and freeze. Makes about 3 quarts.

For 6 servings, use 1½ quarts of the meat sauce. Cook

½ pound spaghetti *al dente,* about 12 minutes, in a large amount of boiling salted water. Turn out on a platter or individual plates, spoon hot meat sauce over, and sprinkle with cheese.

🦋

When available, fresh clams are best in this pasta sauce.

Spaghetti with Clam Sauce / *Spageto me Kydonia*

    2 dozen clams (little neck or rock), or 2 cans
         (8 ounces *each*) minced clams
    ½ cup dry white wine
    ½ cup water
    Salt
    ¼ cup butter
    1 medium-sized onion, finely chopped
    2 cloves garlic, minced
    ½ teaspoon dried oregano
    ½ teaspoon dried basil
    1 can (8 ounces) tomato sauce
    2 tablespoons finely chopped fresh parsley
    12 ounces spaghetti
    Freshly grated Parmesan or Romano cheese

If using fresh clams, scrub them thoroughly under cold running water, using a stiff brush. Place in a kettle, add the wine and water, and sprinkle lightly with salt. Cover and steam for 10 minutes, or until the shells open. Reserve broth. Let clams cool slightly, then remove from shells and chop finely.

If using canned clams, drain and add liquid to wine.

Melt butter in a large frying pan, and sauté onion and garlic until limp. Add oregano, basil, tomato sauce, parsley, and reserved wine broth, and cook down until thickened. Add clams and heat until hot through. Cook spaghetti *al dente*, about 12 minutes, in a large amount of boiling salted water; drain. Turn out on a hot platter, sprinkle with cheese, and pour the clam sauce over. Sprinkle with more cheese on top. Makes 4 servings.

The nutty richness of browned butter makes a flavor-packed coating on spaghetti for a pleasing side dish to roast meats.

Spaghetti with Browned Butter and Parmesan / *Spageto me Fresko Voutiro ke Patmezana*

½ pound spaghetti
½ cup butter
1½ cups freshly grated Romano or Parmesan cheese

Cook spaghetti *al dente*, about 12 minutes, in a large amount of boiling salted water. Drain well and turn out on a large hot platter. Heat butter until it sizzles and turns golden brown, and pour over spaghetti. Sprinkle with cheese and mix lightly. Makes 6 servings.

Feta melts within a golden omelet, providing a creamy rich sauce. Feel free to substitute a mixture of fresh garden herbs, such as chives, marjoram, thyme, or basil, for the oregano. Though this is geared for one, you can turn out a battery of omelets with great dispatch for a family or guest brunch.

Feta Cheese Omelet / *Avga me Feta*

> 3 eggs
> 1 tablespoon water
> ¼ teaspoon salt
> Dash pepper
> 1 tablespoon butter
> ¼ cup crumbled feta cheese
> ¼ teaspoon dried oregano, or 1 teaspoon fresh mixed herbs
> 1 tablespoon minced parsley

For each individual omelet, beat together the eggs, water, salt, and pepper. Heat an 8-inch omelet pan, add butter, and when it stops foaming add eggs all at once. Slip a thin spatula under the eggs just as soon as they set, and lift to let the uncooked eggs flow underneath. Sprinkle cheese and oregano or fresh herbs on top, and when set, but still creamy, fold over and turn out of pan. Sprinkle with parsley. Serves 1.

This vegetable omelet closely resembles the Italian frittata. Other vegetables, such as leeks, mushrooms, or zucchini, can replace the artichokes.

Artichoke Omelet / *Avga me Anginares*

> 1 package (8 ounces) frozen artichoke hearts, thawed
> 2 green onions, chopped
> ¼ cup butter
> 3 tablespoons dry white wine
> 6 eggs
> Salt and pepper
> 2 tablespoons finely chopped parsley
> 2 tablespoons shredded Romano or Parmesan cheese

Using a large frying pan, sauté artichoke hearts and onions in 2 tablespoons of the butter for a few minutes. Add wine, cover, and simmer 5 minutes, or until artichokes are tender. Add remaining butter to pan. Beat eggs with salt and pepper to taste until light. Pour into pan and cook over low heat, without stirring, until eggs are set. Slide onto a platter and sprinkle with parsley and cheese. Cut in wedges. Serves 3 or 4.

SEAFOOD

If you can get it, "live" crab is excellent simmered in this fashion, letting its juices exude into the tomato wine sauce.

Stewed Crab / *Kavoura Yahni*

    2 bunches green onions, chopped (use only part of the green tops)

    ¼ cup olive oil

    1 can (8 ounces) tomato sauce

    ⅓ cup pale dry sherry

    ½ teaspoon salt

    2 cloves garlic, minced

    ½ teaspoon dried basil or oregano

    1¼ pounds Dungeness crab meat or canned Alaska King crab meat, or 1 large crab, cleaned and cracked

    2 tablespoons finely chopped parsley

    1 lemon, cut in wedges

In a large frying pan, sauté onions in oil until golden brown. Add tomato sauce, sherry, salt, garlic, and basil or oregano. Cover and simmer 15 minutes. Add crab and heat for 5 to 10 minutes, or until hot through. Sprinkle with parsley. If desired, serve over pilaf and garnish with lemon wedges. Serves 4.

🦂

In Greece and the islands, lobster is a local treat frequently listed on restaurant menus. The tiny imported Iceland lobster tails (just 3 inches long and ¾ inch wide) are a delicacy to prepare in this manner.

Boiled Lobster / *Astakos Vrastos*

    2 small lobsters, split in half, or 4 lobster tails
    Court bouillon
    ⅓ cup olive oil
    3 tablespoons lemon juice
    1 tablespoon minced parsley
    1 tablespoon chopped fresh chives or green onions
    ½ teaspoon salt
    Freshly ground pepper

In a large kettle simmer lobsters in court bouillon just until tender, about 5 to 10 minutes depending on size; drain. Mix together in a small bowl the olive oil, lemon juice, parsley, chives or onions, salt, and pepper. Loosen the lobster meat at the end of the tail and lift out; slice into pieces 1 inch thick and return to the shell. Spoon the lemon dressing over the lobster and chill before serving. Serves 4.

🦂

At the waterfront tavernas in Piraeus, this is a celebrated seafood casserole. Ouzo imbues the shrimp with an enticing anise overtone. Pilaf is a proper accompaniment, along with crusty sesame-coated bread and a dry white wine.

Shrimp with Feta / *Garides me Feta*

    3 tablespoons lemon juice
    2 pounds medium-sized raw shrimp, shelled and
      deveined
    1 medium-sized onion, finely chopped
    1 bunch green onions, finely chopped (use only
      part of green stems)
    1 clove garlic, minced
    ⅓ cup olive oil
    1 can (15 ounces) tomato purée
    ½ cup dry white wine
    ½ cup clam juice
    2 tablespoons butter
    2 tablespoons ouzo or Pernod
    1 teaspoon dried oregano
    2 tablespoons finely chopped fresh parsley
    ½ pound feta cheese, cut in ½-inch squares

Pour lemon juice over cleaned shrimps and let stand while preparing sauce. In a large frying pan, sauté onions and garlic in oil. Add tomato purée, wine, and clam juice, and let simmer, uncovered, 15 minutes.

In another frying pan, sauté shrimp in butter until they turn pink. Heat ouzo or Pernod, ignite, and spoon flaming over the shrimp. Mix shrimp, oregano, and parsley into the sauce. Spoon into a buttered baking dish or individual ramekins and scatter feta cheese over the top, pushing it in slightly. Bake in a 375° oven for 15 minutes, or until hot through and cheese starts to melt. Serves 4.

✤

Skewered broiled shrimp make a striking entrée on a dinner plate. Accompany with pilaf to capture the rich juices, and fresh asparagus or zucchini.

Broiled Shrimp / *Garides tis Skaras*

½ cup olive oil or butter, melted
¼ cup lemon juice
3 tablespoons dry vermouth
4 cloves garlic, minced
2 tablespoons finely chopped parsley
1 green onion, finely chopped
2 teaspoons dried oregano
Salt and freshly ground pepper
2 pounds extra-large raw shrimp, shelled and
    deveined (12 count to a pound)
1 lemon, cut in wedges

Combine in a large bowl the oil or butter, lemon juice, vermouth, garlic, parsley, onion, oregano, and salt and pepper to taste; stir just until blended. Add shrimp and let marinate at room temperature 1 hour. Thread shrimp on skewers and place on a broiler pan. Broil on both sides, basting with the marinade, allowing about 5 to 7 minutes, or until shrimp turn pink. Serve with pan juices spooned over. Garnish with lemon. Makes 4 servings.

✤

Bright coral shrimp nestle in a bed of butter-browned pilaf.

Shrimp Pilaf / *Garides Pilafi*

    2 cups court bouillon (or 1 cup *each* clam juice
       and water)
    2 pounds medium raw shrimp
    1 medium onion, finely chopped
    1 bunch green onions, finely chopped (use only
       part of green stems)
   ½ cup finely chopped celery
   ⅓ cup olive oil
    1 cup long-grain rice
    2 tablespoons tomato paste
    3 tablespoons finely chopped fresh parsley
    1 teaspoon dried oregano
   ¼ cup butter

    In a large pan bring the court bouillon or clam broth to a boil. Add the raw shrimp, cover, and simmer 5 to 7 minutes, or until shrimp turn pink. Drain and reserve 2 cups liquid. Let shrimp cool, then peel and devein.

    In a Dutch oven or flameproof casserole, sauté onions and celery in oil until vegetables are glazed and limp. Add the rice and stir until oil-coated. Add tomato paste and reserved broth. Cover and simmer for 20 minutes. Arrange shrimp on top of the rice and sprinkle with parsley and oregano. Heat butter until it bubbles and browns slightly, and immediately pour over the shrimp and rice. Cover and let stand 5 minutes. Serves 4 to 6.

CRAB VARIATION. Substitute 1 pound fresh or canned Dungeness or Alaska King crab meat for the shrimp in the recipe above. Use clam juice and water for broth and add the crab meat directly to rice the last 5 minutes, just to heat through.

🦟

Most any kind of fish steak is excellent with skordalia *as a dressing.*

Fish Steaks with Garlic Mayonnaise / *Psari me Skordalia*

2 pounds halibut, swordfish, or salmon steaks, cut about ¾ inch thick
3 tablespoons butter, melted
1 tablespoon lemon juice
Salt and pepper
Lemon wedges
Skordalia: garlic mayonnaise with pine nuts or almonds (see page 126)

Place fish steaks on a broiling pan and brush with a mixture of melted butter and lemon juice. Broil, turning to brown both sides and basting several times, allowing about 10 to 12 minutes, or until fish flakes with a fork. Sprinkle with salt and pepper to taste. Place on a serving plate and garnish with lemon wedges. Pass *skordalia* in a bowl, or fill small clam shells for individual servings and arrange alongside each fish steak. Makes 6 servings.

🦟

This colorful skewered fish entrée alternates swordfish or halibut, cherry tomatoes, and feathers of bay. Greeks would pass more lemon and oregano at the table, letting each person further season his own souvlakia.

Fish on Skewers / *Psari Souvlakia*

¼ cup olive oil
⅓ cup dry vermouth
3 tablespoons lemon juice
½ teaspoon salt
1 teaspoon dried oregano
2 cloves garlic, minced
1 green onion, finely chopped
2 pounds swordfish or halibut steaks, cut ¾ inch thick
1½ cups cherry tomatoes
1½ dozen fresh bay leaves (optional)
1 lemon, cut in wedges
Oregano

Mix together in a bowl the oil, vermouth, lemon juice, salt, oregano, garlic, and onion. Cut fish steaks into 1 ¼-inch squares, place in the marinade, cover, and chill several hours, turning once or twice.

Alternate on skewers the fish chunks, tomatoes, and bay leaves (if used). Place on a broiler pan and broil about 10 minutes, turning to brown both sides and basting with marinade. (Or barbecue over medium-hot coals.) Accompany with lemon wedges and a dish of oregano. Serves 6.

When you have access to freshly caught trout at the beach or mountains, cook it this neat, compact way.

Trout in Parchment / *Psari Sto Harti*

3 green onions, finely chopped
¼ cup butter
¼ pound fresh mushrooms, chopped
1 clove garlic, minced
2 tablespoons chopped parsley
4 trout, cleaned (about 6 to 8 ounces each)
4 zucchini, thinly sliced
Salt and pepper
½ teaspoon oregano
2 tablespoons lemon juice
2 tablespoons olive oil
1 lemon, thinly sliced

In a frying pan, slowly sauté onions in butter until limp. Add mushrooms and sauté just until glazed. Remove from heat and stir in garlic and parsley. Wash trout and pat dry; stuff each fish with the sautéed vegetable mixture and place each on an oiled piece of parchment or double square of foil. Arrange sliced zucchini alongside each fish. Sprinkle with salt and pepper to taste, oregano, lemon juice, and oil. Arrange 1 or 2 lemon slices on each fish. Bring up parchment or foil and fold tightly at top and ends to seal. Place on a baking sheet and bake at 400° for 15 to 20 minutes, or until fish flakes with a fork. If desired, remove from packets before serving. Serves 4.

Fish steaks, sandwiched between a thick bed of sautéed vegetables, acquire a tantalizing succulence as they oven bake.

Baked Fish with Vegetables / *Psari Plaki Tourlou*

2 bunches green onions, chopped
2 stalks celery, finely chopped
4 small carrots, peeled and thinly sliced
⅓ cup olive oil
1 pound fresh spinach, chopped
½ cup finely chopped fresh parsley
1 can (6 ounces) tomato sauce
2 cloves garlic, minced
Salt and freshly ground pepper
2½ pounds halibut or sea bass steaks, cut 1 inch thick
Lemon wedges

In a large frying pan, sauté onions, celery, and carrots in oil until oil-glazed. Add the spinach, parsley, tomato sauce, garlic, and salt and pepper to taste. Cover and simmer 15 minutes. Spoon half the vegetable mixture into a buttered baking pan; cover with fish steaks and spoon remaining vegetable mixture on top. Cover and bake in a 350° oven for 45 minutes, or until the fish flakes when tested with a fork. Serve with lemon wedges. Makes 8 servings.

A simple lemon and herb dressing laves fish with a piquant zest.

Broiled Fish with Lemon Sauce /
Psari tis Skaras me Saltsa Politiki

2 pounds Greenland turbot or sole fillets or salmon or halibut steaks

3 tablespoons melted butter

Salt and pepper

¼ cup olive oil

3 tablespoons lemon juice

3 tablespoons finely chopped fresh parsley

1 green onion, chopped

1 teaspoon dried oregano

Place fish steaks on a broiling pan, brush with melted butter, and sprinkle with salt and pepper to taste. Broil on both sides, brushing with butter. Broil about 8 minutes for the turbot or sole, and 10 to 12 minutes for salmon or halibut, or cook until fish flakes when tested with a fork. Meanwhile combine in a small bowl the oil, lemon juice, parsley, onion, and oregano, and beat with a fork just until blended. Place fish on a hot platter and pour the lemon and herb sauce over. Makes 6 servings.

A *vinegar sauce, aromatic with rosemary and browned gar-lic nuggets, permeates fish fillets to lend distinction whether served hot or cold. Years ago the cooking method was devised to preserve fish, thus the name* psari marinata, *or marinated fish.*

Marinated Fish / *Psari Marinata*

2 pounds Greenland turbot fillets, sole fillets, or halibut steaks
Flour seasoned with salt and pepper
¼ cup olive oil
¼ cup white wine vinegar
4 cloves garlic, minced
2 teaspoons fresh rosemary, or ½ teaspoon dried rosemary

Dip fish fillets in the seasoned flour, coating both sides lightly. Heat oil in a large frying pan, and sauté the fish, turning to brown both sides. Remove to a hot platter. Add vinegar, garlic, and rosemary to pan. Stirring, scrape up the drippings and let cook down slightly. Spoon over fish and serve hot or chilled. Makes 6 servings.

POULTRY
AND GAME

This fragrant stuffing is an exotic melding of meats, nuts, and vegetables.

Roast Stuffed Turkey / *Galopoulo Yemistos*

20-pound (approximately) turkey
⅓ cup lemon juice
Salt and pepper
1 pound chestnuts
1 pound lean ground beef
Turkey liver, or ½ pound chicken livers, chopped
½ cup butter
2 large onions, finely chopped
2 medium-sized carrots, finely chopped
2 stalks celery, chopped
2 teaspoons poultry seasoning
1 teaspoon cinnamon
½ teaspoon nutmeg
½ cup pine nuts
2 cups crushed zwieback crumbs
8 eggs

Wash turkey thoroughly and wipe dry. Rub the entire surface as well as the cavity with lemon juice, salt, and pepper.

For stuffing, cut a ½-inch slit in the side of each chestnut. Place in a saucepan, add enough boiling water to cover, and simmer 10 minutes. Drain, then peel and chop. Using a large Dutch oven, sauté ground beef and chopped livers in 3 tablespoons of the butter, stirring, until meat is browned. Push to sides of pan, add remaining butter and onions, and sauté until golden. Add the chopped chestnuts, carrots, celery, poultry seasoning, cinnamon, and nutmeg, and simmer 2 hours (if necessary, add ½ cup water). Add pine nuts and simmer 15 minutes longer. Remove from heat and let the mixture cool slightly. Mix in the crushed zwieback crumbs. Beat the eggs until light, and stir into the stuffing mixture.

Stuff turkey loosely and truss. Insert a meat thermometer in a thigh. Place in a shallow roasting pan, pour in 1 cup water, and bake in a 325° oven until the thermometer registers 185°, or about 4½ hours, basting frequently. Makes about 18 to 20 servings.

Note: If you use a smaller turkey, bake any extra stuffing in a covered pan at 325° for 1 hour.

A whole bird roasts to a beautiful brown and then gets a finishing splash of lemon juice. Vegetables such as potatoes, mushrooms, and artichokes may cook in the pan juices.

Roast Chicken / *Kota Psito*

1 large broiler-fryer (about 3½ pounds)
2 tablespoons butter
1 teaspoon salt
1 teaspoon dried oregano
Freshly ground pepper
2 cloves garlic, minced
⅓ cup lemon juice
½ cup water

Wash chicken well and pat dry. Melt butter in a roasting pan and roll chicken in the butter, turning to coat all sides. Mix together the salt, oregano, pepper, and garlic, and rub the surface of the chicken and the cavity with these seasonings. Place bird breast side up and roast in a 425° oven for 25 to 30 minutes, or until golden brown. Reduce heat to 325° and continue roasting 1 hour longer, or until the leg joint moves easily. Remove from oven. Pour lemon juice over the chicken, transfer to a hot platter, and cover loosely with foil. Skim fat from the pan drippings and stir in the water; bring to a boil and pour into a sauce boat. Carve chicken and pour over sauce. Serves 4 to 6.

VEGETABLE ACCOMPANIMENTS TO ROAST CHICKEN. Peel 4 medium-sized potatoes and cut in lengthwise wedges. Roll in melted butter and place in the pan at the beginning of roasting. Or add ½ pound small mushrooms to pan juices the last 30 minutes of roasting. Or add 1½ pounds parboiled small artichoke hearts to the pan juices the last 30 minutes of cooking.

🏶

The name Plaka denotes the colorful taverna section in Athens, a hillside area that comes to life at night with music and dining, where this dish is a specialty. Pilaf studded with pine nuts and raisins roasts inside broiler-fryers.

Roast Chicken Plaka Style / *Kota Plaka*

2 whole broiler-fryer chickens (about 3 pounds *each*), or 1 roasting chicken (5 to 5½ pounds)
Salt and pepper
1 teaspoon grated lemon peel
2 cloves garlic, minced
1 cup long-grain white rice
2 cups chicken broth
1 medium-sized onion, finely chopped
½ cup butter
⅓ cup golden raisins or currants
½ cup pine nuts or slivered almonds
1 cup dry white wine
1 can (15 ounces) artichoke hearts, or 16 parboiled fresh tiny artichoke hearts

Wash chicken and giblets and pat dry. Rub with salt, pepper, and lemon peel. Tuck garlic inside chicken cavities. Steam rice in the broth for 20 minutes. Meanwhile, in a large frying pan, sauté onion in 2 tablespoons of the butter. Chop the chicken livers and add to onion along with raisins and nuts; sauté a few minutes, add to rice, and fluff lightly with a fork. Heat remaining butter until it sizzles and starts to brown, then pour over rice; fluff with a fork. Spoon stuffing inside birds and place breast side up in a large roasting pan. Tuck remaining giblets alongside.

Roast in a 425° oven for 25 minutes. Reduce temperature to 350° and pour the wine over the chicken. Continue roasting 1 hour longer (or 1½ hours for the roasting chicken). Add artichokes to pan juices, cover with foil, and roast 15 minutes longer, or until the leg joints move easily. Transfer to a large carving board and surround with artichokes. Skim fat off pan juices, and pour juices into a sauce bowl. Makes about 8 servings.

Herbs and lemon juice permeate chicken parts as they marinate and broil.

Broiled Chicken Oregano / *Kotopoulo Riganato*

> 3-pound broiler-fryer, cut in pieces, or chicken
>   parts (breasts, thighs, drumsticks)
> ¼ cup lemon juice
> 3 tablespoons olive oil
> 1 teaspoon dried oregano
> 2 cloves garlic, minced
> Salt and freshly ground pepper
> ¼ cup butter, melted
> 1 lemon
> Oregano

Wash chicken pieces and pat dry. Place in a large shallow bowl. Mix together the lemon juice, olive oil, oregano, garlic, and salt and pepper to taste, and pour over chicken; cover and chill several hours, turning occasionally. To cook, place on a broiler rack or on a barbecue grill over hot coals and brush with melted butter. Add remaining marinade to butter. Basting chicken several times, broil about 15 minutes on each side, or until chicken is richly browned. Serve with lemon wedges and a small dish of oregano to sprinkle over as desired. Makes 4 to 6 servings.

This entrée parallels the classic beef stew of the same name. There is plenty of spicy tomato sauce—ideal for drenching pilaf or noodles.

Chicken with Onions / *Kotopoulo Stifado*

    3-pound broiler-fryer chicken, cut in pieces
    3 tablespoons butter
    1 medium-sized onion, chopped
    1 teaspoon mixed pickling spice
    1 can (6 ounces) tomato paste
    3 tablespoons white wine vinegar
    1½ cups chicken stock
    2 cloves garlic, minced
    Salt and pepper
    1 pound small white onions

Wash chicken and pat dry. Melt butter in a Dutch oven and sauté onion until golden. Add chicken pieces and sauté until browned. Tie pickling spice in a cheesecloth bag, and add to chicken along with tomato paste, vinegar, stock, garlic, and salt and pepper to taste. Cover and simmer 20 minutes. Peel onions and cut a small cross in the root end of each one to prevent them from bursting. Add to the stew and simmer 25 minutes longer, or until onions are tender. Remove pickling spice, and skim fat from pan juices. Serve chicken and onions along with the sauce. Makes 4 to 6 servings.

CHEESE VARIATION. The last 15 minutes of cooking, ¼ pound Kasseri or Romano cheese, cut in cubes, may be added.

🦂

Nuggets of Greek cheese heat to a melting richness in the spicy sauce for braised chicken.

Chicken with Cheese / *Kotopoulo me Teri*

    3-pound broiler-fryer, cut in pieces
    3 tablespoons butter or olive oil
    1 medium-sized onion, chopped
    Salt and pepper
    1 clove garlic, minced
    3 tablespoons tomato paste
    1 stick cinnamon
    1 bay leaf
    1 cup chicken stock
    ⅓ pound Kasseri or Romano cheese, cut in ¾-
        inch cubes
    Pilaf

Wash chicken pieces and pat dry. Heat butter or olive oil in a large Dutch oven or frying pan. Add chicken pieces and brown on all sides. Add onion and sauté until golden.

Add salt and pepper to taste, garlic, tomato paste, cinnamon stick, bay leaf, and chicken stock; cover and simmer for 35 minutes, or until almost tender. Add cheese and cook 10 minutes longer. Remove cinnamon stick and bay leaf before serving. Serve with pilaf. Makes 4 to 6 servings.

🐟

This is a popular basic chicken recipe to which various vegetables are often added. In addition to artichokes, potatoes, green beans, boiling onions, eggplant, and new peas are favorites.

Chicken and Artichoke Stew / *Kota me Anginares Yahni*

> 3-pound broiler-fryer, cut in pieces, or chicken
>   parts
> 1 medium-sized onion, chopped
> 3 tablespoons butter
> Salt and pepper
> 2 cloves garlic, minced
> 1 can (15 ounces) whole peeled tomatoes
> 3 tablespoons tomato paste
> ¼ teaspoon cinnamon
> 1 cup chicken stock
> 4 medium-sized artichokes, or 1 package
>   (8 ounces) frozen artichoke hearts, thawed
> 2 tablespoons lemon juice

Wash chicken and pat dry. Using a Dutch oven, sauté onions in butter until golden; push to sides of pan. Add chicken pieces and sauté until golden brown, turning. Add salt and pepper to taste, garlic, tomatoes, tomato paste, cinnamon, and chicken stock. Cut the tops off the artichokes, if you are using fresh ones, and peel off the tough outer leaves. Cut in half, scrape out the center chokes, and sprinkle with lemon juice. Add to the pan. Cover and simmer for 45 minutes, or until chicken and artichokes are tender. If you are using artichoke hearts, omit lemon juice and add them the last 10 minutes of cooking. Skim any fat from the sauce. Makes 4 to 6 servings.

🦐

The classic refreshing lemon sauce binds chicken and vegetables for this succulent one-dish meal. You may substitute various quick-cooking or parboiled vegetables such as mushrooms, artichoke hearts, zucchini, or Italian green beans. If you wish to make this dish in advance, prepare it just to the point before adding the egg-lemon sauce. Once that is blended in, the sauce is likely to curdle if reheated.

Chicken with Lemon Sauce / *Kota Avgolemono*

　　3-pound broiler-fryer, cut in pieces
　　2 tablespoons butter
　　2 cloves garlic, minced
　　Salt and pepper
　　1 cup chicken stock
　　1 pound crookneck squash, sliced
　　1½ cups fresh shelled peas, or 1 package
　　　　(10 ounces) frozen petit peas, thawed
　　2 eggs
　　2 tablespoons lemon juice
　　½ teaspoon oregano

Using a frying pan or Dutch oven with cover, brown chicken on all sides in butter. Add garlic, salt and pepper to taste, and chicken stock; cover and simmer 25 minutes. Add squash and peas, and simmer 10 minutes longer. Skim any fat from the pan juices.

For sauce, beat together the eggs and lemon juice. Slowly pour in the pan juices, beating constantly with a wire whisk. Return to pan and place over very low heat until sauce thickens, stirring occasionally (do not boil). Serve chicken and vegetables in the sauce, sprinkled with oregano. Makes 4 to 6 servings.

Browned butter saturates pilaf with a rich nuttiness and golden hue. The chicken acquires a gentle spiciness during braising.

Chicken Pilaf with Browned Butter / *Kotopoulo Pilafi*

3-pound broiler-fryer, cut in pieces
½ cup butter
1 large onion, finely chopped
1 teaspoon salt
Freshly ground pepper
½ teaspoon cinnamon
Dash allspice
1 clove garlic, minced
3 tablespoons tomato paste
1 cup chicken stock
1 cup long-grain white rice
½ pint yogurt
1 tablespoon finely chopped fresh mint (optional)

Wash chicken and pat dry. Using a large Dutch oven, sauté chicken pieces in 3 tablespoons of the butter, turning to brown all sides. Add onion and sauté until golden. Add salt, pepper, cinnamon, allspice, garlic, and tomato paste, and cook 2 or 3 minutes longer, stirring frequently. Pour in chicken stock, cover, and simmer for 45 minutes, or until chicken is tender; remove chicken from pan and keep warm. Pour off pan juices and measure; you should have 2 cups. If necessary add water or reduce quickly to make that amount. Pour juices back into the pan and bring to a boil; add rice, cover, and simmer 20 minutes, or until rice is tender. Heat the remaining butter until bubbly and lightly browned in color and pour over rice, tossing lightly with a fork. Return chicken to the pan to heat through. Serve with a side dish of yogurt, mixed with mint, if desired. Serves 4 to 6.

🦂

This handsome chicken breast entrée is a specialty of a fashionable Greek restaurant that presents native food in a gala style. Baby asparagus spears are effective here.

Chicken Olympus / *Kota Olympus*

    3 whole chicken breasts (about 2½ pounds), split
       (6 pieces)
    ¼ cup butter
    Salt and pepper
    1 clove garlic, minced
    ⅓ cup dry white wine
    ⅓ cup chicken stock

1 pound fresh small asparagus spears
½ pound small fresh mushrooms
Hot cooked rice or pilaf
Avgolemono sauce (see below)

Using a large frying pan, sauté chicken in 2 tablespoons of the butter, turning to brown both sides. Season with salt, pepper, and garlic. Cover pan and cook over medium heat for 10 minutes. Pour in wine and chicken stock and let simmer 15 minutes longer, or until tender. Pour off chicken stock and reserve for sauce; keep chicken warm.

Trim ends of asparagus and leave whole; cook in boiling salted water for 5 to 7 minutes, or until tender; drain. Sauté mushrooms in the remaining butter. Spoon a ribbon of rice onto 6 dinner plates; arrange a chicken breast alongside and lay a bundle of asparagus crosswise on the chicken. Spoon *avgolemono* sauce on top, and scatter mushrooms over. Serves 6.

AVGOLEMONO SAUCE. Measure out 1 cup reserved pan juices (if necessary, add water or cook down to make 1 cup). Pour into a saucepan and bring to a boil. Blend together 1 tablespoon cornstarch and 1 tablespoon cold water and stir in; stirring, cook until thickened. Beat 2 egg yolks until light, and stir in ½ cup whipping cream. Pour hot sauce into egg yolk mixture, stir to blend, and return to the saucepan. Place over very low heat and cook until thickened, stirring constantly. Blend in 1½ tablespoons lemon juice just before serving.

For a cool entrée, a garlic-nut mayonnaise is an inviting dressing on chicken breasts.

Chicken Breasts with *Skordalia* / *Kota me Skordalia*

3 large whole chicken breasts (about 2½ pounds), split (6 pieces)
2 tablespoons butter
Salt and pepper
½ cup chicken stock
½ teaspoon dried marjoram or tarragon
1 egg
2 cloves garlic, minced
½ teaspoon salt
1½ tablespoons lemon juice
1½ tablespoons white wine vinegar
¾ cup salad oil (or part olive oil)
½ cup chopped walnuts or almonds (toasted, if desired)
Cherry tomatoes
Cucumber sticks
Watercress

In a large frying pan, sauté chicken breasts in butter until golden brown. Add salt and pepper to taste, chicken stock, and marjoram or tarragon; cover and simmer 15 minutes, or until meat is white through. Remove from broth and let cool; chill. (Use broth for another purpose.)

Meanwhile, for *skordalia*, break egg into the blender container and add garlic, salt, lemon juice, and vinegar. Blend a few seconds. With motor running, gradually pour in oil and blend until smooth. Add nuts and blend a few seconds. Empty into a bowl, cover, and chill.

To serve, arrange chicken on a platter or individual plates, and garnish with cherry tomatoes, cucumber sticks, and watercress. Pass *skordalia* to spoon over. Makes 6 servings.

🐾

Homemade yogurt is generally used for this chicken entrée. Undertones of cinnamon and lemon peel refresh the sauce.

Chicken with Yogurt / *Kota me Yiaourti*

 3-pound broiler-fryer, cut in pieces
 1 medium-sized onion, finely chopped
 2 tablespoons butter
 2 cloves garlic, minced
 Salt and pepper
 1 teaspoon grated lemon peel
 ½ cup chicken broth
 ½ cup dry white wine or vermouth
 1 stick cinnamon
 2 tablespoons cornstarch
 1½ cups yogurt
 Hot pilaf
 Dolmathes (page 44)

Wash chicken and pat dry. In a Dutch oven sauté onion in butter until golden; push to sides of pan and sauté chicken pieces until golden brown. Add the garlic, salt and pepper to taste, lemon peel, broth, wine, and cinnamon stick. Cover and simmer for 40 minutes. Remove cover and bring broth to boiling. Blend cornstarch with 2 tablespoons cold water, and stir into broth. Cook until thickened, stirring. Stir part of the hot sauce into the yogurt; return to pan and heat over very low heat until hot through. Serve over pilaf and garnish with *dolmathes*. Makes 4 to 6 servings.

🦋

Like the cheese and meat bourekakia, *these chicken rolls freeze well. For a buffet party, you might offer a selection of several kinds of fila rolls for an easy-to-manage, intriguing entrée.*

Chicken and Mushroom Fila Rolls / *Kota Bourekakia*

 1 medium-sized onion, finely chopped
 1 bunch green onions, chopped (use only part of green stems)
 ½ cup butter
 ¼ pound fresh mushrooms, chopped
 1 barbecued or roasted broiler-fryer (about 3 pounds)
 ¼ cup finely chopped fresh parsley
 Dash nutmeg
 3 eggs
 2 cups (½ pound) shredded Gruyère or Samsoe cheese
 14 to 16 sheets prepared fila dough

Using a large frying pan, sauté onions in 2 tablespoons of the butter until limp. Add mushrooms and sauté until glazed; let cool. Remove skin and bones from chicken, and cut meat into bite-size pieces (you should have 4 cups meat). Place chicken in a bowl and add sautéed vegetables, parsley, nutmeg, eggs, and cheese; mix well.

Melt remaining butter. Lay out one sheet of fila (keep remaining fila covered with clear plastic wrap), brush half with melted butter, fold sheet in half, making a 9-by-12-inch rectangle. Brush again with butter, and spoon about ⅓ cup of the chicken mixture along one end. Fold in the long sides about 1¼ inches and roll up, making a roll about 6½ inches long and 1½ inches wide. Place seam side down on a lightly greased baking sheet. Repeat. Bake in a 350° oven for 20 to 25 minutes, or until golden brown. Makes 14 to 16 rolls.

🦅

In Athenian restaurants where businessmen dine this is a familiar luncheon entrée. A 4- to 5-pound stewing hen, simmered until tender, may be substituted for the broiler-fryers.

Chicken Pita / *Kota Pita*

- 2 barbecued or roasted broiler-fryers
- 1 cup butter
- 1½ pounds mushrooms, sliced
- 1 bunch green onions, chopped
- ½ cup double-strength chicken broth
- ½ cup dry white wine
- 2 tablespoons chopped fresh parsley
- Salt and pepper
- 4 eggs, beaten
- 1 tablespoon minute tapioca
- 1 cup (4 ounces) shredded Gruyère or Samsoe cheese
- 12 sheets prepared fila dough (about ⅓ pound)

Remove skin and bones from cooked chicken, and dice meat (you need about 8 cups). Melt ½ cup butter in a large frying pan, and sauté mushrooms and onions just until glazed. Pour in chicken broth and wine, and boil down rapidly until liquid is practically gone; let cool. Add chicken, parsley, salt and pepper to taste, beaten eggs, tapioca, and cheese, and mix lightly.

Melt remaining butter. Lay out fila dough and cover with clear plastic film to keep from drying out. Line a buttered 9-by-13-inch baking pan with 6 sheets of fila, brushing each sheet lightly with melted butter and letting fila overlap the sides of pan. Spoon in chicken and mushroom mixture, spreading it evenly. Fold in any fila which overlaps. Cover with remaining fila sheets, cut or folded in to fit pan, brushing each with melted butter. With a razor blade or sharp knife, cut through the top of the fila sheets, making 2¼-inch pieces. Bake in a 350° oven for 45 minutes, or until the top is golden brown and filling is set. Place on a rack and let cool slightly. Cut through completely. Serve warm or at room temperature. Makes about 24 pieces or 12 servings.

The zest of citrus enhances broiled game hens. In Greece partridges or quail might substitute for these domestic birds.

Game Birds with Oranges / *Kotopoulo me Portokali*

2 Rock Cornish game hens (about 20 to 24 ounces *each*)
Salt and pepper
¼ cup butter
1 tablespoon lemon juice
1 teaspoon grated lemon peel
½ teaspoon dried oregano or tarragon
1 clove garlic, minced
2 tablespoons honey
2 oranges, sliced ½ inch thick with peel on
Watercress or parsley

Wash hens well and pat dry. Using poultry shears or kitchen scissors, cut hens in half lengthwise. Sprinkle the surface with salt and pepper, and arrange on a rack in a broiler pan with skin side down. In a small pan heat together the butter, lemon juice, peel, oregano or tarragon, and garlic; brush over the hens. Broil about 6 inches from the heat, turning once and basting several times, for about 25 minutes or until the leg joint moves easily. Drizzle honey over the orange slices and broil just until heated through and browned. Arrange birds on a serving platter and garnish with hot orange slices and watercress or parsley. Serves 4.

MEATS

Celebrating the holiday feast out of doors with music and dancing is an important Easter tradition. A whole kid or baby lamb is spit-roasted for the event. It is wise to order the kid (a young goat) or lamb well in advance from a Greek or Italian butcher. Have the meat prepared for roasting.

Kid or Lamb on a Spit / *Katsikakaia e Arni tis Souvlas*

    1 kid or baby lamb (about 10 pounds)
    Salt and pepper
    6 cloves garlic, minced
    2 tablespoons dried oregano
    2 teaspoons dried thyme
    1 cup lemon juice
    1 cup olive oil

Wash and pat dry the kid or lamb and rub it well with salt, pepper, and garlic. Mix together the oregano, thyme, lemon juice, and oil, and rub part of it over the meat; reserve remaining sauce for basting. Insert meat on a spit and bring up the rear and front legs, tying them to the spit. Cook meat on a revolving spit over medium coals, basting occasionally with the lemon sauce, allowing about 3 to 4 hours, depending on the weight of the animal and heat of the coals. Makes about 10 to 12 servings.

The classic Greek way with leg of lamb is notable for its simplicity and succulence. The garlic, herbs, and lemon penetrate the meat and the pan juices for a fine treat. For ease in carving, the meat may be boned, rolled, and tied before roasting.

Roast Leg of Lamb / *Arni Psito*

1 leg of lamb (6 to 7 pounds)
4 cloves garlic
2 teaspoons salt
½ teaspoon freshly ground pepper
2 teaspoons dried oregano
¼ cup lemon juice
Garnish: fresh rosemary sprigs, lemons, oregano

Trim any extra fat from the meat. Peel garlic and sliver it. Insert several garlic slivers in the natural seams of the meat and make additional incisions and insert more garlic. Mix together the salt, pepper, and oregano, and poke half of the mixture into the slits. Rub remaining salt mixture over the outside of the meat. Insert meat thermometer in the thickest part of the roast.

Place on a rack in a roasting pan and pour ½ cup hot water into the bottom of the pan. Place in a 400° oven and roast for 40 minutes, or until the meat is well browned. Reduce temperature to 325° and roast 1 to 1½ hours longer or until the thermometer registers 160° for medium-rare meat (still slightly pink inside). (Boned and tied lamb will take slightly longer than bone-in lamb.) Remove from oven.

Pour lemon juice over the meat, cover pan, and let stand 10 minutes. Remove meat from pan to a platter and keep warm. Skim fat from pan juices and pour 1 cup water into the pan; stirring, bring to a boil, scraping up drippings. Pour into a sauce bowl. Garnish meat platter with a wreath of rosemary. Cut lemons in half, zigzag style, sprinkle their center with oregano, and arrange on the rosemary. Carve lamb, and spoon juices over each serving. Makes about 10 to 12 servings.

Butterflied lamb is the meat market term for a leg of lamb which has been boned and laid open flat. In this form it is easy to barbecue on the grill. Certain sections will be thicker than others, so try to adjust the heat of the coals accordingly.

Butterflied Barbecued Lamb / *Arni Roti*

    1 leg of lamb (6 to 7 pounds), boned and
       butterflied
    ¼ cup lemon juice

¼ cup dry vermouth
3 tablespoons olive oil
2 teaspoons salt
½ teaspoon freshly ground pepper
2 teaspoons dried oregano
½ teaspoon dried thyme
½ teaspoon dried rosemary
4 cloves garlic, minced
Lemons
Citrus leaves (optional)

Lay out the meat in a large shallow pan or casserole. Mix together the lemon juice, vermouth, oil, salt, pepper, oregano, thyme, rosemary, and garlic, and pour over the meat. Turn meat to coat both sides, and chill several hours, or preferably overnight.

Barbecue meat on a grill over medium-hot coals, allowing about 20 minutes to brown one side; turn to brown other side, cooking about 20 minutes more for medium-rare meat. Baste several times during grilling with marinade. Place on a carving board and garnish with lemon wedges and citrus leaves, if available. Slice to serve. Makes about 10 servings.

*Lemon and oregano are used freely with meats for season-
ing. Here they lend a sprightliness to broiled or barbecued
lamb steaks.*

Broiled Lamb Steaks / *Paidakia tis Scaras*

  6 lamb steaks, cut 1 inch thick
  ½ cup dry white wine or vermouth
  3 tablespoons lemon juice
  ¼ cup olive oil
  2 cloves garlic, minced
  1 teaspoon oregano
  ½ teaspoon salt
     Freshly ground pepper
  1 lemon, cut in wedges

Trim any extra fat from the meat. Mix together the wine,
lemon juice, oil, garlic, oregano, salt, and pepper. Place
steaks in a large shallow dish, pour the marinade over them,
and turn to coat meat well. Cover and chill, marinating
several hours or overnight, turning occasionally. Broil or
barbecue over medium-hot coals, turning meat once, and
basting with remaining marinade. Allow about 15 minutes
for rare steaks. Garnish with lemon wedges. Serves 6.

Souvlakia stands abound in Greece where one can buy skewers of barbecued lamb to tuck inside a soft pita bun and eat sandwich fashion on the street. This version is like one you might sample in a restaurant or home.

Lamb on Skewers / *Arni Souvlakia*

3 pounds boneless leg of lamb, cut in 1½-inch cubes
⅓ cup lemon juice
3 tablespoons olive oil
1 teaspoon salt
1 teaspoon dried oregano
2 cloves garlic, minced
1 small onion, grated
¼ teaspoon freshly ground pepper
2 green peppers, cut in 1½-inch pieces
1 large white onion, cut in eighths

Place meat in a bowl. Mix together the lemon juice, oil, salt, oregano, garlic, grated onion, and pepper, and pour over meat. Cover and chill several hours, or preferably overnight, turning several times.

Thread meat on skewers, alternating on each one about 4 or 5 lamb cubes, 2 pieces of green pepper, and 1 piece of onion. Barbecue over medium-hot coals, basting often with marinade and turning to brown on all sides, allowing about 15 minutes for medium-rare meat. Makes 8 servings.

VARIATION. Substitute 2 dozen small boiling onions for the large onion and green peppers. Peel onions and cut a small cross in the root end of each to prevent bursting. Parboil for 10 minutes in boiling salted water; drain, then thread on skewers with meat.

🦎

To conceal their whereabouts from the Turks, the Greeks years ago cooked their meat wrapped in paper, known as kleftiko. Foil provides a fine substitute today. The packets make a fascinating dinner party surprise.

Lamb Chops in a Jacket / *Arni Psito Sto Charti*

6 large loin lamb chops
1 teaspoon salt
1 teaspoon oregano
Freshly ground pepper
2 cloves garlic, minced
6 small zucchini, halved
6 small yellow crookneck squash, halved
1 bunch green onions, chopped
¼ pound Kasseri or feta cheese, cut into 6 squares
3 tablespoons lemon juice
¼ cup butter, melted
Salt and pepper

Season each chop with a mixture of salt, oregano, pepper, and garlic. Place each chop on a large double square of foil, and lay 2 zucchini halves and 2 crookneck squash halves on each. Scatter onions on top, and add a square of cheese. Drizzle vegetables with lemon juice and butter, and sprinkle them lightly with salt and pepper. Fold the squares of foil into a double fold at the top and sides; secure sides with paper clips. Place packets in a baking pan and bake in a 350° oven for 1 hour, or place packets on a grill over charcoal and cook, turning once, 1 hour, or until tender. Remove clips and place sealed packets on dinner plates. Or, if desired, remove from foil before serving. Serves 6.

🐝

Another version of cooking lamb "bandit style" is done here in a paper bag. White or brown bags, lunch bag size, work fine; just be certain to coat the bags completely with vegetable oil before baking (this prevents them from scorching). Each bag holds dinner for one.

Lamb Shanks Bandit Style / *Arni Kleftiko*

    6 lamb shanks (with bones uncracked)
    1½ teaspoons salt
    1½ teaspoons dried oregano
    4 cloves garlic, minced
    1 teaspoon grated lemon peel
    Freshly ground pepper
    1 dozen small boiling onions
    6 small carrots
    18 fresh mushrooms, about 1¼-inch size
    ¼ cup melted butter
    1 green onion, finely chopped
    2 tablespoons chopped parsley
    6 heavy-duty paper bags, about 6 inches across
        bottom
    Salad oil

With a sharp knife make several small slits in each lamb shank. Mix together the salt, oregano, garlic, lemon peel, and pepper to taste, and poke half the mixture into the slits.

Rub remaining mixture on the outside of the shanks. Peel onions and make a small cross in the root end of each one to keep the insides from popping out. Peel carrots and cut off ends. Clean mushrooms. Mix together in a bowl the melted butter, chopped onion, and parsley, and roll vegetables in the seasoned butter, coating completely.

Cut 3 inches off the tops of the bags and rub the outside of bags with oil, coating completely. Place in each bag 2 onions, 1 carrot, and 3 mushrooms. Place a seasoned lamb shank on top of each vegetable medley. Fold down tops of bags and secure sides with paper clips. Place bags on a baking pan and bake in a 325° oven for 2 hours, or until meat is tender. Use a spatula to transfer bags to dinner plates. Serves 6.

🦅

Sizzling browned butter lends a marvelous nutty finish and keeps each rice grain separate in this lamb pilaf.

Lamb with Rice / *Arni Pilafi*

> 2 pounds boneless lamb leg or shoulder, cut in
>   1½-inch pieces
> 2 medium-sized onions, chopped
> 10 tablespoons butter
> 2 cloves garlic, minced
> 2 tablespoons tomato paste
> 1 tablespoon chopped parsley
> ¼ teaspoon cinnamon
> Salt and pepper
> 2 cups meat stock
> 1 cup long-grain white rice
> Freshly grated Parmesan or Romano cheese

Using a Dutch oven or flameproof casserole, sauté meat and onions in 2 tablespoons of the butter until browned. Add garlic, tomato paste, parsley, cinnamon, salt and pepper to taste, and stock. Bring to a boil, cover, and simmer for 45 minutes to 1 hour, or until meat is almost tender. Add rice, stir, and simmer for 20 minutes, or until liquid is absorbed. Heat remaining butter until sizzling and lightly browned, pour over meat and rice, fluff with a fork, cover, and let stand for 10 minutes. Serve with cheese to sprinkle over the top. Makes 6 servings.

Kapama is the Greek word for braising meat or poultry with onions, tomatoes, and cinnamon, and incorporating macaroni. Beef or veal may replace the lamb.

Lamb with Macaroni / *Arni Kapama*

    2 pounds boneless stewing lamb, cut in 1½-inch
       pieces
    2 medium-sized onions, finely chopped
    10 tablespoons butter
    Salt and pepper
    2 cloves garlic, minced
    ½ stick cinnamon
    ¼ cup tomato paste
    1 can (15 ounces) tomato purée
    1 cup meat stock
    2 teaspoons brown sugar
    ¼ cup white or red wine vinegar
    1 teaspoon mixed pickling spice
    12 ounces macaroni
    Freshly grated Parmesan or Romano cheese

Using a large Dutch oven, brown meat and onions in 2 tablespoons of the butter. Add salt and pepper to taste, garlic, cinnamon stick, tomato paste, tomato purée, meat stock, sugar, and vinegar. Tie pickling spice in cheesecloth or place in tea ball, and add to liquid. Bring to a boil, cover, and simmer for 1 hour, or until meat is tender. Remove cinnamon stick and pickling spice. Meanwhile, cook macaroni *al dente* in boiling salted water; drain well. Turn out on a heated platter. Heat remaining butter until bubbly and golden brown, pour over macaroni, and mix lightly. Spoon part of the sauce from the meat over macaroni, and sprinkle generously with cheese. Pass meat with sauce separately. Makes 6 to 8 servings.

🎚

A Greek pasta such as orzo or manestra is proper for this oven-baked entrée. Fashionable Athenian tavernas like to serve giouvetsi *in individual earthenware casseroles.*

Lamb with Pasta / *Giouvetsi*

2 tablespoons butter
2 pounds boneless lamb leg or shoulder, cut in 1½-inch pieces
1 medium-sized onion, chopped
2 cloves garlic, minced
Salt and pepper
½ cup dry white wine or vermouth
3 tablespoons tomato paste
3 cups meat stock
12 ounces orzo or manestra
Freshly grated Parmesan or Romano cheese

Melt butter in a large flameproof casserole (such as a paella pan) or roasting pan. Add meat, onion, and garlic, and turn until coated with butter. Season with salt and pepper. Place in a 450° oven and roast for 20 minutes, or until meat is browned. Reduce temperature to 325°, add wine, tomato paste, and 1 cup stock; continue baking 40 minutes longer. Add remaining stock to pan juices.

Meanwhile, parboil pasta in a large amount of boiling salted water for 5 minutes; drain well and add to the sauce in the roasting pan. Stir, and continue baking for 30 minutes, or until pasta is *al dente* and the meat is tender. Serve meat and pasta in hot individual casseroles (or a large casserole) and sprinkle with cheese. Makes 6 to 8 servings.

🦂

Freshly chopped tomatoes, stirred in at the last, lend a cool juiciness to this hot white bean stew.

Lamb with White Beans / *Kreas me Fasolia*

12 ounces dried small white beans or Great Northern beans
2 pounds boneless lamb stew, cut in 1½-inch pieces
3 tablespoons olive oil
2 medium-sized onions, finely chopped
1 stalk celery, finely chopped
4 medium-sized carrots, peeled and sliced
2 teaspoons salt
3 tomatoes, peeled
Freshly ground pepper
1 teaspoon oregano

Cover beans with water and bring to a boil. Cook 2 minutes, cover, and let stand 1 hour; drain. Using a Dutch oven, brown meat in oil, turning to brown all sides. Add onion and celery, and sauté until limp. Add drained beans, carrots, salt, and enough water to cover meat and beans. Cover and simmer 2 hours, or until beans and meat are tender. Chop tomatoes and add to stew along with freshly ground pepper to taste and oregano. Serve at once. Makes 6 to 8 servings.

※

This basic stew is the starting point for half a dozen versions with various vegetables.

Lamb Stew / *Arni Yahni*

> 2 pounds boneless lamb, cut in 1½-inch pieces
> 1 tablespoon butter
> 1 large onion, finely chopped
> 2 cloves garlic, minced
> 2 medium-sized tomatoes, peeled and chopped, or 1 can (8 ounces) tomato sauce
> 1 cup water or dry white wine
> 2 teaspoons salt
> Freshly ground pepper

Using a large Dutch oven, brown meat in butter, turning to brown all sides. Add onion and sauté until limp. Add garlic, tomatoes, water or wine, salt, and pepper to taste. Cover and simmer for 1½ hours, or until meat is tender. Makes 6 servings.

Lamb Stew with Artichokes / *Arni Yahni me Anginares*

Follow the basic recipe for lamb stew. Add 2 packages (8 ounces *each*) frozen artichoke hearts and ½ teaspoon oregano or dill to stew the last 15 minutes of cooking. Or if desired use 6 fresh artichokes. Wash and clean artichokes, peeling off the tough outer leaves, cut in half, and scoop out center choke with a spoon; rub with lemon juice. Add to the stew along with oregano or dill the last 40 minutes of cooking. Makes 6 servings.

Lamb Stew with Eggplant / *Arni Yahni me Melitzana*

Follow the basic recipe for lamb stew. Peel 1 large eggplant (about 1½ pounds) and cut into 1½-inch cubes. Add to the meat the last 30 minutes of cooking. Sprinkle with 2 tablespoons parsley. Makes 6 servings.

Lamb Stew with Green Beans / *Arni Yahni me Fassoulakia*

Follow the basic recipe for lamb stew. Wash and trim ends from 1½ pounds green beans; cut in half lengthwise. Parboil in boiling salted water for 10 minutes; drain. Add beans and ½ teaspoon oregano to the stew the last 20 minutes of cooking. Or if desired, add 2 packages (9 ounces each) frozen Italian-style green beans, thawed. Do not parboil; add to the stew the last 20 minutes of cooking. Makes 6 servings.

Lamb Stew with Potatoes / *Arni Yahni me Patates*

Follow the basic recipe for lamb stew. Wash and peel 4 to 6 medium-sized potatoes. After browning the meat, add potatoes to the stew along with ½ teaspoon cinnamon. Cover and simmer for 1½ hours, or until meat and potatoes are tender. Makes 6 servings.

Lamb Stew with Zucchini / *Arni Yahni me Kolokithia*

Follow the basic recipe for lamb stew. Wash and trim ends from 1½ pounds zucchini and cut into 1-inch pieces. Sauté zucchini in 1 tablespoon butter just until lightly browned, and add to the stew along with ½ teaspoon oregano the last 20 minutes of cooking. Sprinkle with 2 tablespoons chopped parsley. Makes 6 servings.

Lamb Stew with Vegetables / *Arni Yahni me Tourlou*

Follow the basic recipe for lamb stew. Wash and trim ends from ½ pound green beans; cut in half lengthwise. Peel and cut 6 small carrots in half lengthwise. Cut 3 zucchini in 1-inch pieces. Add vegetables to the stew the last 20 minutes of cooking. Makes 6 servings.

Lemon and dill bring out the best in this likable Greek stew.

Lamb with Celery, Lemon Sauce /
Arni me Selino, Avgolemono

> 2 pounds boneless lamb, cut in 1½-inch cubes
> 2 tablespoons butter
> 1 medium-sized onion, finely chopped
> Salt and pepper
> ½ teaspoon dried dill
> 1 cup water
> 3 celery hearts
> *Avgolemono* sauce (see page 125)

Using a Dutch oven or flameproof casserole, sauté lamb in butter until meat is browned. Add onion and sauté until golden. Season with salt and pepper to taste and dill. Pour in the water and let cook a few minutes, scraping up the drippings. Cover and simmer for 1½ hours, or until meat is almost tender.

Wash and trim celery hearts and cut in half lengthwise. Add to meat and simmer for 15 minutes, or until tender. Prepare 1 recipe of *avgolemono* sauce, and slowly stir sauce into the stew. Heat gently (without boiling) until thickened. Makes 6 servings.

Lamb with Broccoli, Lemon Sauce / *Arni me Brokola Avgolemono*

Follow the recipe above for lamb with celery, but omit celery hearts and substitute 1 large bunch broccoli. Wash and trim ends; cut into flowerets. Add to meat and simmer for 10 minutes, or until tender. Makes 6 servings.

Lamb with Squash and Lemon Sauce / *Arni me Kolokethia Avgolemono*

Follow the recipe above for lamb with celery but omit celery hearts and substitute 1½ pounds zucchini or yellow crookneck squash. Wash squash and trim off ends; cut in ¾-inch slices. Add to meat and simmer for 10 minutes, or until tender. Makes 6 servings.

A beef chuck or rump is a fine cut to pot-roast. Accompany with mashed potatoes or rice to absorb the savory pan juices.

Beef Pot Roast / *Vothino Entrada*

4-pound beef pot roast
2 teaspoons salt
¼ teaspoon pepper
2 tablespoons flour
2 tablespoons butter
3 medium-sized onions, thinly sliced
½ cup dry red wine
2 tablespoons tomato paste
1 bay leaf
1 stick cinnamon
Finely chopped fresh parsley

Rub meat with salt, pepper, and flour. Using a Dutch oven, brown meat in butter on both sides. Add onions and sauté until limp. Add wine, tomato paste, bay leaf, and cinnamon stick; cover and simmer for about 2 hours, or until meat is tender when pierced with a fork. Place meat on a board, sprinkle with parsley, and slice. Skim fat from sauce and remove bay leaf and cinnamon stick. Pass sauce separately. Makes about 8 to 10 servings.

The zest of lemon and garlic lends finesse to steak, either broiled or barbecued.

Grilled Beef Steak / *Brizoles Vothines Sti Skara*

> 1½ to 2 pounds sirloin steak or top round, cut about 1¼ inches thick
> Salt
> Freshly ground pepper
> 1 clove garlic, minced
> 3 tablespoons lemon juice
> 1 teaspoon dried oregano
> 1 lemon, cut in wedges

Season meat with salt and pepper and rub with garlic. Broil or barbecue over medium-hot coals, turning once, until browned yet still pink inside, about 15 minutes. Place on a carving board and sprinkle with lemon juice and oregano. Slice into strips or cut into serving-size pieces. Garnish with lemon wedges. Makes about 4 to 6 servings.

This classic stew is scented with pickling spice and punctuated with wine vinegar. Serve with a ring of sesame-coated Greek bread and a dry red wine or retsina.

Beef and Onion Stew / *Stifado*

2 pounds stewing beef, cut in 1½-inch pieces
2 tablespoons butter
2 teaspoons salt
3 cloves garlic, minced
1 teaspoon mixed pickling spice
1 stick cinnamon
¾ cup dry red wine
3 tablespoons red wine vinegar
3 tablespoons tomato paste
1 tablespoon brown sugar
1½ pounds small whole onions
2 tablespoons currants (optional)
2 tablespoons finely chopped fresh parsley

Using a Dutch oven or flameproof casserole, brown meat in butter, turning to brown all sides. Season with salt and garlic. Place mixed pickling spice and cinnamon stick in a cheesecloth bag or tea ball and add to the meat. Pour in wine and add vinegar, tomato paste, and brown sugar. Cover and simmer 1 hour. Peel onions and cut a small cross in the root end of each one to prevent them from bursting. Add onions and currants (if desired) to the stew and simmer 30 minutes longer, or until onions and meat are tender. Sprinkle with parsley. Makes 6 servings.

(continued)

NUT AND CHEESE VARIATION. If desired, ½ cup walnut halves and ⅓ pound feta or Monterey Jack cheese, cubed, may be added the last 5 minutes of cooking.

🐝

Lemon sauce makes a tangy backdrop for rice-plumped meatballs.

Meatballs with Lemon Sauce / *Youvarlakia Avgolemono*

1½ pounds lean ground beef
3 tablespoons finely chopped parsley
1 small onion, grated
1 clove garlic, minced
2 teaspoons finely chopped mint
¼ cup long-grain white rice
1½ teaspoons salt
Pepper
2 cups beef stock
2 tablespoons flour
2 eggs
1 tablespoon cornstarch
3 tablespoons lemon juice

For meatballs, mix together the ground beef, parsley, onion, garlic, mint, rice, salt, pepper to taste, and ⅓ cup of the beef stock. Shape into 1¼-inch balls and roll in flour. Heat the remaining beef stock to boiling, add meatballs, cover, and simmer 35 minutes, or until rice is tender.

Beat eggs until blended, then beat in cornstarch and lemon juice. Gradually pour in the broth from the meatballs and whisk lemon-egg mixture until blended. Return sauce to the meatballs and heat over very low heat for a few minutes, just until sauce is thickened. Makes 4 to 6 servings.

꽃

Smyrna is credited with these sausage-shaped meat patties that simmer in a spicy tomato sauce. You may use ground beef, pork, or veal, or a mixture of these. Accompany with pilaf, noodles, or macaroni.

Smyrna Meat Sausage / *Smyrnaika*

Tomato sauce (see below)
2 slices white bread, crumbled
⅓ cup dry red or white wine
1½ pounds ground beef, pork, or veal
2 eggs
2 tablespoons chopped parsley
2 cloves garlic, minced
1½ teaspoons salt
¼ teaspoon ground cumin
¼ teaspoon ground cinnamon
Freshly ground pepper
Flour
¼ cup butter
Freshly grated Parmesan or Romano cheese

Prepare tomato sauce (see below). While it simmers, soak crumbled bread in wine, then place in a mixing bowl with ground meat, eggs, parsley, garlic, salt, cumin, cinnamon, and pepper. Mix thoroughly and shape into finger-length sausages. Roll in flour and brown in butter, turning to brown all sides. Pour in the tomato sauce, cover, and simmer 15 minutes. Serve with freshly grated cheese. Makes 4 to 6 servings.

TOMATO SAUCE. Place in a saucepan 1 can (6 ounces) tomato paste, 1 cup dry red wine, 1 cup water, 1 tablespoon brown sugar, 1 clove garlic, minced, ½ teaspoon salt, and pepper to taste. Cover and simmer 30 minutes.

For a delightful, novel luncheon or supper entrée, serve these meat-and-cheese-filled fila diamonds. Good companions are a country salad with feta and tomatoes, crusty sesame-coated bread, and lemon ice with strawberries.

Meat-Filled Pie / *Kreatopita*

3 medium-sized onions, finely chopped
10 tablespoons butter
1½ pounds ground beef
1½ pounds ground veal or pork
3 cloves garlic, minced
2 teaspoons salt
1 teaspoon dried oregano
Freshly ground pepper
1 can (8 ounces) tomato sauce
½ cup dry red wine
3 eggs, slightly beaten
3 tablespoons chopped fresh parsley
1½ cups freshly grated Parmesan or Romano
cheese

2 slices white bread, crumbled
12 sheets prepared fila dough

Using a large frying pan, sauté onion in 2 tablespoons of the butter until golden; remove and set aside. Add ground meats to pan and sauté until browned. Add sautéed onion, garlic, salt, oregano, pepper, tomato sauce, and wine; simmer, uncovered, stirring occasionally, for 20 minutes, or until liquid evaporates. Remove from heat and let cool slightly. Mix in eggs, parsley, grated cheese, and bread crumbs.

Melt remaining butter. Lay out fila and cover with clear plastic film. Line a buttered 9-by-13-inch baking pan with 6 sheets of fila, brushing each sheet lightly with melted butter and letting fila overlap the sides of pan. Spoon in ground meat and cheese mixture, spreading it evenly. Fold in any fila which overlaps. Cover with remaining fila sheets, cut or folded in to fit pan, brushing each with melted butter. With a razor blade or sharp knife make lengthwise cuts 2 inches apart through the top layer of fila, then cut across diagonally, making diamonds about 2 inches wide and 3 inches long. Bake in a 350° oven for 45 minutes, or until the top is golden brown and filling is set. Place on a rack and let cool slightly. Cut through completely. Serve warm or at room temperature. Makes about 24 pieces or 12 servings.

A crispy fila wrapper encircles meat loaf, transforming it into party fare.

Fila Meat Roll / *Bourekakia me Kreas*

1 medium-sized onion, chopped
2 tablespoons butter
3 eggs
⅔ cup milk
1½ cups soft white or French bread crumbs
2 teaspoons salt
Freshly ground pepper
2 cloves garlic, peeled
2 teaspoons Worcestershire sauce
2 tablespoons chopped fresh parsley
1½ pounds lean ground beef
1 pound ground pork
8 sheets (¼ pound) prepared fila dough
Melted butter
Yogurt mixed with chopped green onion
   (optional)

Sauté onion in butter until golden; set aside. In a blender container place eggs, milk, bread crumbs, salt, pepper to taste, garlic, Worcestershire, and parsley, and blend until smooth. Empty into a bowl, add the sautéed onion and ground meats, and mix thoroughly until blended. Pat into a 4-by-12-inch log and place on a lightly greased baking pan. Bake in a 375° oven for 35 minutes; let cool.

Lay out fila and cover with clear plastic film. Brush one sheet with melted butter and arrange remaining buttered sheets of fila on top overlapping, to make a rectangle about 15 by 20 inches. Place meat loaf across a narrow side and roll up. Tuck in ends. Place on a greased baking sheet and brush with melted butter. Bake in a 375° oven for 20 minutes or until fila is crispy and brown. Transfer to a cutting board or platter. Cut into l-inch slices. If desired, serve with yogurt blended with green onion. Makes 8 to 10 servings.

🜲

In Greece you'll find that moussaka often comes with an extra-thick, pasty custard topping as high as the layers beneath, and it's shy on meat sauce. This version is more refined. Other vegetables can replace the eggplant; note the variations below.

Moussaka

Meat sauce (see below)
2 large eggplants, unpeeled
6 tablespoons olive oil
½ cup butter
½ cup flour
1 quart milk
1 teaspoon salt
⅛ teaspoon nutmeg
⅛ teaspoon pepper
5 eggs
¼ cup fine dry bread crumbs
1 cup freshly grated Parmesan cheese

First prepare meat sauce (see next page).
Slice eggplants ¾ inch thick. Place on 2 well-oiled 10-by-15-inch baking pans and coat both sides of eggplant with

the oil. Bake in a 400° oven for 30 minutes, or until tender, turning once.

Melt butter and blend in flour, gradually stir in milk and, stirring constantly, cook until thickened. Season with salt, nutmeg, and pepper. Beat eggs until light, and blend the hot sauce into them.

Arrange half the eggplant in a greased 9-by-13-inch baking pan. Mix meat sauce with crumbs and spread half over the eggplant. Sprinkle with half the cheese. Cover with another layer of eggplant and remaining meat sauce. Spoon custard sauce over the top, and sprinkle with cheese. Bake in a 350° oven for 50 minutes to 1 hour, or until set and lightly browned. Let stand 10 to 15 minutes, then cut into squares. Makes about 12 servings.

MEAT SAUCE. Using a large frying pan, sauté 2 pounds lean ground beef in 2 tablespoons butter until meat is browned and crumbly. Add 2 medium-sized onions, finely chopped, and sauté until golden. Add 3 tablespoons tomato paste, ½ cup dry red wine, 3 tablespoons minced parsley, 2 teaspoons salt, freshly ground pepper, ¼ teaspoon cinnamon, ¼ teaspoon allspice, and 2 cloves garlic, minced. Cover and simmer 45 minutes (sauce should be very thick).

ZUCCHINI VARIATION. Instead of the eggplant, substitute 2 pounds zucchini. Trim ends from the squash and slice lengthwise or on the diagonal about ⅓ inch thick. Sauté in the olive oil, turning, until crisp tender. Continue with basic moussaka recipe above.

(continued)

POTATO VARIATION. Instead of the eggplant, substitute 2 pounds potatoes, peeled and sliced ¼ inch thick. Sauté in ½ cup butter instead of olive oil until golden brown. Continue with basic moussaka recipe above.

🦐

Veal mingles with onions and mushrooms in a spicy tomato sauce. Accompany with pilaf and a crusty bread.

Veal Ragout with Onions / *Moskari Stifado*

2 pounds boneless veal stew, cut in 1½-inch cubes
4 tablespoons butter
1 medium-sized onion, finely chopped
½ cup tomato sauce
½ cup water
2 tablespoons red wine vinegar
½ teaspoon allspice
2 cloves garlic, minced
2 teaspoons salt
Freshly ground pepper
1½ pounds small white onions
½ pound fresh mushrooms

Using a Dutch oven or flameproof casserole, sauté meat in 2 tablespoons of the butter, turning to brown all sides. Add chopped onion and sauté until golden. Add tomato sauce, the water, vinegar, allspice, garlic, salt, and pepper to taste. Cover and simmer 1 hour. Peel onions and cut a small cross in the root end of each one to prevent them from bursting. Add to the stew and simmer 20 minutes. Clean and halve mushrooms, and sauté in the remaining butter; add to stew and simmer 5 minutes longer. Serves 6.

🦁

Quinces are commonplace in Greece and often paired with veal. Here you may substitute firm winter pears, such as the pale green Anjou or tapering golden russet-colored Bosc.

Veal with Quince / *Moskari me Kidonia*

2 pounds boneless veal stew, cut in 1½-inch pieces
¼ cup butter
1 medium-sized onion, chopped
2 teaspoons salt
Freshly ground pepper
1 clove garlic, minced
1 stick cinnamon
1 cup water
4 quinces or winter pears
½ teaspoon grated lemon peel
1 tablespoon brown sugar
1 tablespoon lemon juice

In a Dutch oven or flameproof casserole, sauté meat in 2 tablespoons of the butter, turning to brown all sides. Add onion and sauté until golden. Add salt, pepper to taste, garlic, cinnamon stick, and the water; cover and simmer 1 hour, or until meat is almost tender. Meanwhile, halve, core, and slice quinces or pears and sauté in remaining butter in a large frying pan. Sprinkle with lemon peel and brown sugar, and cook until fruit is glazed and starts to soften. Arrange on top of the meat, sprinkle with lemon juice, and simmer 15 minutes longer, or until meat is tender. Serves 6.

🜂

A ground ham and mushroom loaf, lemon-scented, bakes between fila for a decorative meat pie. Cut in diamonds, the loaf makes an easy-to-serve buffet party entrée.

Ham-Filled Pie / *Zampon Pita*

    2 medium-sized onions, finely chopped
    10 tablespoons butter
    ⅓ pound fresh mushrooms, finely chopped
    3 pounds lean ground cooked ham or canned
        ham (about 6 cups, lightly packed)
    1½ teaspoons grated lemon peel
    3 eggs
    2 cups (½ pound) shredded Gruyère or Samsoe
        cheese
    2 tablespoons finely chopped fresh parsley
    2 slices white bread, crumbled
    ¼ teaspoon nutmeg
    Salt and pepper
    12 sheets prepared fila dough

Using a large frying pan, sauté onions in 2 tablespoons of the butter until limp and golden. Add mushrooms and sauté just until glazed; let cool slightly. Mix together thoroughly the ham, lemon peel, eggs, cheese, parsley, bread

crumbs, nutmeg, salt and pepper to taste, and sautéed vegetables.

Melt remaining butter. Lay out fila and cover with clear
plastic film. Line a buttered 9-by-13-inch baking pan with
6 sheets of fila, brushing each sheet lightly with melted
butter and letting fila overlap the sides of pan. Spoon in
ground ham and cheese mixture, spreading it evenly. Fold
in any fila which overlaps. Cover with remaining fila sheets,
cut or folded in to fit pan, brushing each with melted butter. With a razor blade or sharp knife make lengthwise cuts
2 inches apart through the top layer of fila, then cut across
diagonally, making diamonds about 2 inches wide and 3
inches long. Bake in a 350° oven for 45 minutes, or until
the top is golden brown and filling set. Place on a rack and
let cool slightly. Cut through completely. Serve warm or
at room temperature. Makes about 24 pieces or 12 servings.

🦋

*When a loin of pork is roasted, potatoes are often added to
the pan, absorbing the rich lemon-scented juices as they
bake.*

Roast Pork Loin / *Hirino Psito*

> 3½- to 4-pound pork loin
> 1½ teaspoons salt
> 1 teaspoon oregano
> 1 clove garlic, minced
> 4 to 6 medium-sized potatoes, peeled and cut in
>   lengthwise strips
> 1½ cups water
> 3 tablespoons lemon juice

Rub meat with salt, oregano, and garlic. Place on a rack in a shallow roasting pan, insert a meat thermometer, and bake in a 325° oven for 1 hour. Place potato strips in the pan, add the water, and sprinkle lemon juice over the meat; continue roasting until meat thermometer registers 175°, about 1 to 1½ hours longer. Transfer meat to a carving board, and serve potatoes and pan juices in a casserole alongside. Makes 6 to 8 servings.

⚜

Pork is less often served in Greece than lamb, veal, or beef. Here is a fine stew pairing it with leeks.

Pork and Leek Stew / *Hirino me Prasa*

2 pounds boneless pork, cut in 1½-inch cubes
1 tablespoon butter
1 medium-sized onion, finely chopped
2 cloves garlic, minced
Salt and pepper
1 tablespoon tomato paste
1 cup water or beef stock
1 bunch leeks (3 to 4 leeks)

Using a Dutch oven or large frying pan, brown meat in butter on all sides. Add onion and sauté until golden brown. Add garlic, salt and pepper to taste, tomato paste, and water or stock; cover and simmer 1 hour. Cut leeks in half lengthwise and wash thoroughly, then cut in ½-inch pieces. Add to meat, and continue cooking 30 minutes longer, or until meat is tender. If necessary, boil down pan juices until reduced and slightly thickened. Makes 6 servings.

SAUCES

Avgolemono *is the piquant golden sauce integral to the Greek cuisine. It laves vegetables, meats, poultry, and fish in a scintillating bath. This sauce is blended into the broth or liquid used to cook the dish it will accompany.*

Egg-Lemon Sauce / *Avgolemono Saltsa*

    3 eggs
    1 tablespoon cornstarch
    ⅓ cup lemon juice
    1 cup broth

    Beat the eggs until blended. Beat in cornstarch and lemon juice. Heat broth or stock to boiling, and slowly pour it into the egg mixture, beating constantly with a wire whisk. Gradually stir this sauce into about 2 cups liquid to be thickened, and cook over low heat, stirring, until sauce coats the spoon (do not boil). Makes about 2 cups sauce.

There are innumerable versions of skordalia, a garlic sauce thickened with potatoes, bread, or nuts. The result is a pungent, thick mayonnaise, outstanding with fish or chicken. It is also excellent as a sauce for cooked vegetables, such as artichoke hearts, eggplant, zucchini, broccoli, or spinach. It makes a fine dip for assorted cold vegetables or smooth spread on cucumber slices topped with shrimp. It is also blended into hearty fish soups. Here are three versions. The first two are typically Greek, rustic in style. The last is refined and most pleasing to all tastes.

Garlic Mayonnaise / *Skordalia*

    1 cup mashed potatoes
    4 cloves garlic, minced
    4 tablespoons white wine vinegar
    ½ teaspoon salt
    ½ cup olive oil

Place in a blender container the potatoes, garlic, vinegar, and salt, and blend until smooth. Slowly add the oil, blending until smooth. Empty into a container, cover, and chill. When ready to serve, the sauce may be diluted with fish or chicken stock or water. Makes about 1½ cups.

Garlic Mayonnaise with Walnuts / *Skordalia me Karidia*

    3 slices white or French bread, crusts removed
    4 cloves garlic, minced
    ¼ cup white wine vinegar
    ½ teaspoon salt
    ½ cup walnuts
    1 cup olive oil

Dip bread in water, just to moisten, then squeeze out any extra liquid; place in a blender container. Add garlic, vinegar, salt, and nuts, and blend until smooth. Gradually add oil, blending until smooth. Empty into a container, cover, and chill. If necessary, thin with fish or chicken stock or water. Makes about 2 cups.

Garlic Mayonnaise with Pine Nuts or Almonds / *Skordalia me Pignalia e Amigthalo*

1 egg
1½ tablespoons lemon juice
1½ tablespoons white wine vinegar
1 teaspoon salt
3 cloves garlic, minced
½ cup olive oil
½ cup salad oil
⅓ cup finely chopped, lightly toasted pine nuts or almonds

Place in the blender container the egg, lemon juice, vinegar, salt, and garlic, and blend a few seconds. With motor running, slowly pour in the olive oil and salad oil. Add nuts and blend a few seconds. Empty into a container, cover, and chill. Makes about 1¼ cups.

Most of the year, canned tomatoes yield a more flavorful sauce than fresh ones. At the height of their season, use fresh tomatoes.

Tomato Sauce I / *Saltsa Domata*

1 small onion, finely chopped
2 tablespoons butter
2 cloves garlic, minced
2 tablespoons chopped fresh parsley
6 ripe, fresh tomatoes, peeled and chopped, or
    1 can (28 ounces) whole, peeled tomatoes
1 teaspoon brown sugar
1 teaspoon dried oregano
½ teaspoon salt
Dash of pepper

Sauté onion in butter in a frying pan. Add garlic, parsley, tomatoes, brown sugar, oregano, salt, and pepper. Simmer, uncovered, for 15 to 20 minutes, stirring with a fork to break up tomatoes. Makes about 3 cups sauce.

Tomato Sauce II / *Saltsa Domata*

1 small onion, finely chopped
2 tablespoons butter
2 cloves garlic, minced
1 can (6 ounces) tomato paste
1½ cups water
½ cup dry red or white wine
1 tablespoon brown sugar
½ teaspoon salt
½ teaspoon cinnamon

Sauté onion in butter in a frying pan. Add garlic, tomato paste, 1½ cups water, wine, brown sugar, salt, and cinnamon. Cover and simmer for 1 hour. Makes about 2 cups sauce.

🦂

Orion, the ancient Greek, is credited with creating the basic white sauce called béchamel. The sauce may be seasoned to suit the appropriate dish, whether for pasta, fish, or fowl.

Béchamel Sauce / *Saltsa Besamel*

¼ cup butter
¼ cup flour
2 cups milk
½ teaspoon salt
Dash of white pepper

Melt butter in a saucepan, add flour, and cook 2 minutes, stirring until smooth. Slowly pour in part of the milk, stirring constantly until smooth and thick. Then pour in remaining milk and cook, stirring constantly, until sauce is smooth and thickened. Season with salt and pepper. Makes 2 cups.

🦂

Yogurt is amazingly simple to make using a few tablespoons of commercial yogurt as a "starter." The product has a flavor identical to the commercial one, but the consistency is generally firmer.

Yogurt / *Yiaourti*

    1 quart homogenized milk
    2 tablespoons yogurt

Pour milk into a saucepan and bring just to a boil; set aside and let cool to 115° (pleasantly warm, but not hot). Blend a few tablespoons of the milk with the yogurt, then stir into the remaining milk. Pour into a small stoneware casserole, crocks, or small jars; cover and place in a warm spot (around 90° to 100°) for 8 to 12 hours, or until set. (Or place in a pan of hot water in a turned-off oven or over a pilot light.) Makes 4 cups yogurt.

BREADS

This big doughnut-shaped yeast bread takes less than two hours from start to finish.

Wreath Bread / *Kouloura*

    2 packages active dry yeast
    ½ cup warm water
    1¾ cups milk, scalded and cooled to lukewarm
    1 teaspoon salt
    2 tablespoons sugar
    3 tablespoons olive oil
    5 cups unsifted all-purpose flour
    1 egg yolk beaten with 1 tablespoon water
    2 tablespoons sesame seed

In the large bowl of your electric mixer, add the yeast to the warm water, and stir to blend. Let stand about 5 minutes, then stir in milk, salt, sugar, and olive oil. Add 3 cups of the flour and beat at medium speed for 5 minutes. Add remaining flour, 1 cup at a time, and beat until smooth. (If necessary, use a wooden spoon to beat in remaining flour.)

Turn out dough onto a lightly floured board and knead for about 5 minutes, or until smooth and no longer sticky (if necessary, knead in extra flour). Cover dough with clear plastic film and let rest 25 minutes.

Knead dough on a lightly floured board to release air bubbles. Then divide dough in half. Knead each portion into a smooth flat ball. With your fingers, poke a hole in the center of each dough round, and pull and stretch dough, making a large doughnut with a center hole about 5 inches in diameter. Place on a greased baking sheet and flatten each loaf to make it about 10 inches in diameter. Cover with clear plastic film and let stand in a warm place for 40 minutes, or until dough feels springy when touched with a finger. Brush loaves with beaten egg yolk mixture, and sprinkle with sesame seed.

Bake in a 350° oven for 35 minutes, or until golden brown. Let cool on racks. Makes 2 large doughnut-shaped loaves.

These chewy flat bread disks actually form a hollow pocket inside when they bake. The dough rounds puff like a balloon and then collapse upon cooling. A very hot oven temperature is essential to their success. In Greece the bread is often used as a bun to enclose souvlakia for an out-of-hand sandwich. Or it is torn into pieces and used as a "pusher" to scoop up dips.

Arabic Bread / *Pita*

  1¼ cups warm water (about 110°)
  1 package active dry yeast

¼ teaspoon sugar
3 cups unsifted all-purpose flour
1 teaspoon salt
2 tablespoons olive oil

Place ¼ cup of the water in a small bowl, add yeast and sugar, stir just to blend, and let stand until dissolved. Place the flour, salt, and oil in a mixing bowl. Add the yeast mixture and remaining 1 cup water and beat with a heavy-duty electric mixer or wooden spoon until flour is completely moistened. Turn out on a lightly floured board and knead until smooth and no longer sticky, about 5 to 10 minutes. Place in a bowl, oil the top lightly, cover, and let rise in a warm place until doubled in size, about 1¼ hours.

Turn out on a lightly floured board and knead lightly to remove air bubbles. Roll into a log 8 inches long and cut into 8 equal pieces. Pat each piece of dough into a ball. Using a rolling pin, roll each ball of dough on the floured board, making a round 6½ inches in diameter and ³/16 inch thick. Place each round on a 6½-inch foil square. Let stand uncovered at room temperature (65° to 70°) for 1 hour.

Place oven rack at lowest slot and heat oven to 500°. Place 4 dough rounds at a time, still on foil, directly on oven rack. Bake about 5 minutes, or until puffed and just starting to brown. Remove from oven and place on cooling racks. Serve while warm, or let cool slightly and slip into plastic bags to stay moist and pliable. If desired, freeze. To serve later, let thaw, stack 4 rounds together, and wrap in foil. Reheat in a 375° oven for 10 to 15 minutes, or until hot through. Makes 8 bread rounds.

A midnight ceremony goes with this bread. It is a custom for the master of the house to slice the loaf as the New Year rings in. The one who finds the baked-in coin is blessed with good fortune in the coming year.

New Year's Bread / *Vasilopeta*

    1 package active dry yeast
    ¼ cup warm water
    ½ cup milk
    ⅓ cup butter
    ½ cup sugar
    3 eggs
    2 teaspoons grated orange peel
    1 teaspoon grated lemon peel
    ½ teaspoon salt
    3¼ cups unsifted all-purpose flour
    1 egg yolk mixed with 1 tablespoon water
    Blanched almonds

Sprinkle yeast into the warm water, stir just to blend, and let stand until dissolved. Heat milk and butter together until butter melts; empty into a mixing bowl and add sugar. Let cool to lukewarm. Add eggs, one at a time, and beat until smooth. Add yeast. Mix in orange peel, lemon peel, and salt. Gradually add 2 cups of the flour and beat for 5 minutes. Gradually add remaining flour, using a heavy-duty electric mixer or wooden spoon.

Turn out dough on a lightly floured board and knead until smooth and no longer sticky, about 5 to 10 minutes. If necessary knead in additional flour. Place dough in a greased bowl, grease the top lightly, cover, and let rise in a warm place until doubled, about 1¼ hours.

Turn out dough on a lightly floured board and knead lightly. If desired, place a silver coin in the dough. Shape into a round cake about 9 inches in diameter, and place on a greased baking sheet. Cover and let rise until doubled, about 40 minutes.

Brush egg yolk mixture evenly over the loaf. Arrange almonds on top forming the numerals of the coming year. Bake in a 325° oven for 40 minutes, or until golden brown. Serve warm. Makes 1 large loaf.

🦂

In this large round holiday sweet bread, the scarlet eggs are placed in the pattern of a cross. (Greek Easter eggs are only red.)

Easter Bread / *Lambropsomo*

  2 packages active dry yeast
  ¼ cup warm water
  ¾ cup milk
  ½ cup butter
  ½ cup sugar
  4 eggs
  1 teaspoon cinnamon
  ½ teaspoon nutmeg
  ½ teaspoon salt
  5 cups unsifted all-purpose flour
  5 hard-cooked eggs, dyed red in the shell
  1 egg white, slightly beaten
  Sesame seeds

Sprinkle yeast into the warm water, stir to blend, and let stand until dissolved. Heat milk and butter together until the butter melts. Pour into a mixing bowl, add sugar, and let cool to lukewarm. Add eggs, one at a time, and beat until smooth. Stir in the yeast mixture, cinnamon, nutmeg, salt, and 2 cups of the flour, and beat at medium speed for 5 minutes. Gradually add remaining flour, using a heavy-duty electric mixer or wooden spoon.

Turn out dough on a lightly floured board and knead until smooth and no longer sticky, about 10 minutes. If necessary, knead in additional flour. Place dough in a greased bowl, grease the top lightly, cover, and let rise in a warm place until doubled, about 1½ hours.

Turn out dough on a lightly floured board and knead lightly. Cut off ⅙ of the dough to use for decoration. Shape remaining dough into a large round loaf, about 10 inches in diameter, and place on a greased baking sheet. Place 1 dyed egg in the center top of the dough, and the other four around the edge, forming tips of the cross. Roll remaining dough into pencil-thin strips and place a cross on top of each egg with the strips, pressing the ends of the strips into the bread to secure the eggs. Cover and let rise until doubled in size. Brush the dough with slightly beaten egg white, and sprinkle with sesame seeds. Bake in a 325° oven for 50 to 55 minutes, or until the loaf sounds hollow when thumped. Serve hot or let cool on a rack. Makes 1 large loaf.

After shaping this braided yeast wreath, it is a Greek tradi-
tion to tuck five red Easter eggs in the crevices, like gems of
a crown. The dough rises, then bakes, sealing the eggs in
place. Do not slice this bread; the strands pull apart easily
for eating.

Easter Twist / *Tsoureki*

<pre>
1   package active dry yeast
¼   cup warm water
½   cup milk
½   cup butter
⅓   cup sugar
3   eggs
½   teaspoon salt
1   teaspoon vanilla
1   teaspoon grated lemon peel
3¼ cups unsifted all-purpose flour
5   hard-cooked eggs, dyed red
1   egg yolk beaten with 1 tablespoon water
3   tablespoons slivered, blanched almonds
</pre>

Sprinkle yeast into the warm water, stir just to blend, and
let stand until dissolved. Scald milk and let cool to lukewarm. Beat butter until creamy, and beat in sugar, eggs,
salt, vanilla, and lemon peel. Stir in yeast mixture and milk.
Gradually add 2 cups of the flour and beat for 5 minutes.
Gradually add remaining flour, using a heavy-duty electric mixer or wooden spoon.

Turn out dough on a lightly floured board and knead
until smooth and no longer sticky, about 5 to 10 minutes.
If necessary knead in additional flour. Place dough in a

greased bowl, butter the top lightly, cover, and let rise in a warm place until doubled, about 1¼ hours.

Turn out dough on a lightly floured board and knead lightly. Divide into 3 equal pieces. Roll and stretch each into a strand about 26 inches long. Place strands parallel and pinch top ends together. Braid. Transfer to a greased baking sheet and form into a wreath. Pinch ends to seal. Press dyed eggs upright in dough at equally spaced intervals. Cover and let rise until doubled, about 40 minutes.

Brush egg yolk mixture evenly over braid without coating eggs. Sprinkle bread with almonds. Bake in a 325° oven for 35 to 40 minutes, or until golden brown. Serve warm, or let cool and reheat. Makes 1 bread ring.

A symbolic cross, shaped of dough and jeweled with walnuts, tops this buttery yeast bread. The anise-scented slices are delicious toasted and spread with butter and honey.

Christmas Bread / *Christopsomo*

- 2 packages active dry yeast
- ½ cup warm water
- ½ cup milk
- ¾ cup butter
- ¾ cup sugar
- 4 eggs
- 2 teaspoons crushed anise seed
- ½ teaspoon salt
- 5 cups unsifted all-purpose flour
- 9 walnut halves
- 1 egg white, slightly beaten

Sprinkle yeast into the warm water, stir to blend, and let stand until dissolved. Heat milk and butter together until butter melts. Pour into a mixing bowl, add sugar, and let cool until lukewarm. Add eggs, one at a time, and beat until smooth. Mix in the yeast mixture, anise seed, salt, and 2 cups of the flour, and beat at medium speed for 5 minutes. Gradually add remaining flour, using a heavy-duty electric mixer or wooden spoon.

Turn out dough on a lightly floured board and knead until smooth and no longer sticky, about 10 minutes. If necessary knead in additional flour. Place dough in a bowl, butter the top lightly, cover, and let rise in a warm place until doubled, about 1½ hours.

Turn out dough on a lightly floured board and knead lightly. Pinch off 2 pieces of dough, each about 3 inches in diameter, and set aside. Shape remaining ball of dough into a smooth flat cake about 9 inches in diameter, and place on a greased baking sheet. Roll each of the small balls into a 14-inch rope, and cut a 5-inch slash in the end of each. Cross ropes on the center of the round loaf. Curl slashed sections away from center, forming a small circle; place a walnut half in each circle, and one in the center of the cross. Brush the loaf with the slightly beaten egg white. Cover loaf lightly, and set in a warm place until almost doubled in size, about 1 hour.

Bake in a 325° oven for 50 to 55 minutes, or until golden brown and the loaf sounds hollow when thumped. Serve hot or let cool on a rack. To serve, cut in half, then cut in ½-inch slices. Makes 1 large loaf.

A *honey butter frosting bakes on this spiral of sweet yeast dough, resulting in a luscious caramelized sheath, crunchy with almonds.*

Honey Coffee Bread / *Melokouloura*

2 packages active dry yeast
½ cup warm water
½ cup butter
¾ cup sugar
1 teaspoon salt
1 teaspoon grated lemon peel
1 teaspoon vanilla
3 eggs
4½ cups unsifted all-purpose flour
1 cup milk, scalded and cooled to lukewarm
Honey topping (see below)
⅓ cup sliced or slivered almonds

Sprinkle yeast into the warm water, stir just to blend, and let stand until dissolved. In a large bowl beat butter and sugar with electric mixer until creamy. Add salt, lemon peel, vanilla, and eggs, beating well after each addition. Add 1 cup flour and beat until smooth. Mix in the yeast mixture and milk. Add 2 cups flour and beat 5 minutes. Gradually add remaining flour, using a heavy-duty electric mixer or wooden spoon.

Turn out on a lightly floured board and knead until smooth and no longer sticky, about 5 to 10 minutes. If necessary, knead in additional flour. Place in a bowl, butter the top lightly, and cover and let rise until doubled in size, about 1 hour and 45 minutes.

Turn out dough and knead lightly on a floured board. Divide dough in half. Shape each piece into a long rope, about 1 inch thick. Place on a greased baking sheet and coil into a spiral, starting in the center. Repeat with remaining dough. Cover and let rise until doubled in size and soft and springy to the touch, about 1 hour and 15 minutes. Spread surface with honey topping and sprinkle with almonds. Bake in a 350° oven for 35 minutes, or until golden brown. Serve warm. If desired, freeze loaves, wrapped airtight. To serve, let thaw and reheat, wrapped in foil, in a 375° oven for 20 minutes. Makes 2 large round loaves.

HONEY TOPPING. Beat together ¼ cup soft butter, ¾ cup confectioner's sugar, 2 tablespoons honey, and 1 egg white.

Athenian bakeries sell these cheese-streaked oval yeast buns for a breakfast snack to eat on the spot.

Cheese Buns "Housekeeping" / *Tiropeta Spitikia*

½ cup butter
¾ cup milk
1 package active dry yeast
3¼ cups unsifted all-purpose flour
1 tablespoon sugar
¼ teaspoon salt
3 eggs
½ pound feta cheese, crumbled

Heat 6 tablespoons of the butter and milk in a saucepan until butter melts; cool to lukewarm. In a large mixing bowl place the yeast, ¾ cup of the flour, sugar, and salt. Pour in the warm butter-milk mixture, and beat until smooth. Add eggs, one at a time, and beat until smooth. Gradually beat in remaining flour, beating well. Turn out on a lightly floured board and knead until smooth and satiny. Place in a bowl, butter the top of dough lightly, cover, and let rise in a warm place until almost doubled in size, about 1½ hours.

Turn out on a lightly floured board and knead lightly. For each bun, cut off a 2¼-inch ball of dough and roll into a 6-inch circle. Sprinkle with 1 tablespoon crumbled cheese. Fold over two opposite sides and pinch together, making tapered ends. Place seam side down on a greased baking sheet; let rise until almost doubled, about 30 minutes. With a wooden skewer or toothpick, prick each bun several times; melt remaining butter and brush over tops of buns. Bake in a 375° oven for 15 minutes, or until golden brown. Makes 16 buns.

DESSERTS

The patrician Greek pastry is undoubtedly baklava, with its many alluring variations. Sometimes almonds or walnuts are used exclusively, while a combination is also excellent. Whole cloves may skewer the diamond layers together, or syrup alone may provide the cohesive. To achieve a crispy, still-moist pastry, it is essential to pour cool syrup over hot pastry, or hot syrup over cool pastry—always have the temperature of the syrup and pastry at opposite extremes. A blender is convenient for grinding the nuts; they should be still slightly coarse, rather than powdery, in texture.

Baklava

Honey syrup (see below)
1 pound (3 cups) almonds, finely chopped or ground
1 pound (4 cups) walnuts, finely chopped or ground
½ cup sugar
2 teaspoons grated lemon peel
2 teaspoons cinnamon
1½ cups unsalted butter, melted
1 pound prepared fila dough

First make honey syrup (see below).

Spread out the nuts in a shallow baking pan and toast in a 300° oven for 10 minutes, or until very lightly browned; let cool. Place the sugar, lemon peel, and cinnamon in a large mixing bowl and mash together with the back of a spoon to blend the citrus oil with the sugar. Add toasted nuts and mix lightly.

Butter a 9-by-13-inch (or 10-by-14-inch) baking pan, and line with 3 sheets of fila, brushing each lightly with melted butter and letting dough overlap sides of pan. Sprinkle lightly with about ½ cup of the nut mixture and repeat, alternating 2 sheets of buttered fila and the nut mixture, ending with fila. Using a razor blade or sharp knife, cut through the top layer of fila, making lengthwise strips 1½ inches wide. Then cut diagonally, making diamonds. Bake in a 325° oven for 1 hour, or until golden brown. Place pan on a rack and cut through diamonds completely, using a sharp knife. Pour the cool honey syrup over baklava. Makes about 4 dozen pieces.

HONEY SYRUP. Combine in a saucepan ¾ cup sugar, ¾ cup water, and 1 stick cinnamon; bring to a boil and boil until clear. Add 1½ cups honey and heat just until blended; then cool. Remove cinnamon stick.

Saragli *is a delectable fila pinwheel, intertwining almonds, walnuts, and pistachios in its honey syrup.*

🐝

Baklava Pinwheels / *Saragli*

Syrup (see below)
½ pound (1½ cups) almonds, very finely
   chopped or ground
½ pound (2 cups) walnuts, very finely chopped or
   ground
⅓ cup sugar
2 teaspoons grated orange peel
1 teaspoon cinnamon
½ pound prepared fila dough (approximately 16
   sheets)
¾ cup unsalted butter, melted
¼ cup chopped pistachios

First make syrup (see below).

Mix together in a bowl the finely chopped nuts, sugar, grated orange peel, and cinnamon. Lay out 1 sheet of fila (keep remaining fila covered with clear plastic wrap) and brush with butter. Fold in half crosswise and brush with butter. Lay another sheet on top, so half of it covers the folded sheet, brush with butter and sprinkle with nuts; fold sheet in half, covering nuts. Repeat, using 8 sheets of fila and half of the nut mixture in all. Starting at a long side, fold in 1 inch to secure nuts in place. Starting at the opposite long side, roll up like a jelly roll. Cut in ¾-inch slices.

Lay rolls on a lightly greased baking sheet, and repeat with remaining fila and nut mixture. Bake in a 350° oven for 25 minutes, or until golden brown.

Pour cool syrup over hot pastries. Spoon pistachios in the center of each pastry at serving time. Makes about 2½ dozen.

SYRUP. Combine ⅓ cup sugar and ⅓ cup water, and boil until clear. Stir in ⅔ cup honey and cool.

🦋

Spicy orange syrup drenches the crispy fila topping and soaks into the farina custard diamonds beneath for this fascinating dessert.

Custard Pastry / *Galatoboureko*

   Syrup (see below)
1 quart milk
¼ cup butter
½ cup sugar
½ cup farina
5 eggs
½ cup orange juice
1 teaspoon vanilla
½ cup unsalted butter, melted
10 sheets prepared fila dough

First make syrup (see below).

In a large saucepan, scald milk, add butter and sugar, and heat until dissolved. Gradually pour in the farina, stirring constantly, slowly bring the mixture to a boil, and re-move from heat. Beat eggs until light, and stir in the farina mixture, the orange juice, and vanilla. Let the custard cool.

Butter a 9-inch-square baking pan and line pan with 1 sheet of fila, letting dough overlap sides of pan. Brush with melted butter, and cover with 4 more sheets of buttered fila. Pour in the cool custard, cover with 1 sheet of fila, cut or folded in to fit top of pan, and brush with melted but-ter. Layer 4 more sheets of fila on top, brushing each with butter and folding in the layers of fila that overlap the sides of the pan. With a razor blade or sharp knife cut through the top layers of fila, making 2¼-inch squares, or cut the layers on the diagonal into diamond shapes.

Bake in a 400° oven for 10 minutes, reduce heat to 350°, and continue baking 45 minutes longer, or until custard is set. Remove pan to a rack and let cool 5 minutes. Slowly pour cool syrup over pastry. Cut into squares or diamonds, following razor lines, and serve warm or cold. Makes 16 pieces.

SYRUP. Place in a saucepan 1½ cups sugar, 1 cup water, 2 teaspoons grated orange peel, and 1 cinnamon stick. Bring to a boil and simmer 5 minutes. Let cool.

During baking, this farina-thickened custard billows up, forming a golden soufflélike topping and lemon-scented custard beneath. It cuts neatly into squares. It is excellent plain. If you like, give it a cinnamon-sugar dusting.

Custard Squares / *Galatopeta*

> 1 quart milk
> 1¼ cups sugar
> ½ cup farina
> ½ cup butter
> 8 eggs, separated
> 2 teaspoons grated lemon peel
> 2 teaspoons vanilla
> Confectioner's sugar and cinnamon (optional)

In a large saucepan, heat milk and 1 cup of the sugar until scalded. Gradually stir in farina and, stirring constantly, cook until thickened, and milk mixture comes to a full rolling boil. Add butter, remove from heat, and stir to blend in butter.

Beat egg whites until soft peaks form, then beat in the remaining ¼ cup sugar. Beat egg yolks until thick and pale, beat in lemon peel and vanilla, then fold into the egg white meringue. Pour in the farina mixture and fold together until blended. Pour into a buttered 9-by-13-inch baking pan and smooth top evenly. Place pan in a larger pan (such as a jelly roll pan) with an inch of hot water. Bake in a 350° oven for 40 minutes, or until golden brown, and a knife inserted in the center comes out clean. Remove to a rack and let cool. If desired, dust lightly with confectioner's sugar and cinnamon. Cut into squares. Makes about 24 pieces.

🦎

Bougatsa *is a fila specialty borrowed from Istanbul. There the custard is flavored with an exotic orange-flavored liqueur called* baharika.

Orange Custard Pastry / *Bougatsa*

2 cups milk
⅓ cup farina
2 eggs
½ cup sugar
1 teaspoon vanilla
1 teaspoon grated orange peel
1 tablespoon Cointreau or undiluted orange juice concentrate, thawed
½ cup unsalted butter, melted
12 sheets prepared fila dough
Confectioner's sugar

Bring milk to a boil and slowly stir in the farina; reduce heat and, stirring constantly, cook until thickened. Beat eggs until light, and beat in the sugar. Add part of the hot farina mixture to the eggs and return to the saucepan. Cook over low heat, stirring, until thickened. Remove from heat and stir in vanilla, orange peel, and liqueur or orange juice; let cool.

Lay out 1 sheet of fila and brush half of it with melted butter. Fold over the second half and brush with melted butter. Spoon a heaping tablespoon of cream filling on the narrow end of the dough, leaving a 1-inch border. Fold over the two long sides 1 inch, and fold up the bottom 1 inch. Then fold over, making 3-inch-wide folds. Place seam side down on a buttered baking sheet. Repeat process for other pastries.

Bake in a 375° oven for 15 to 20 minutes, or until golden brown. Dust tops while hot with confectioner's sugar, and transfer to a rack. Makes 12 pastries.

🦎

For this unique pastry you need kadaife *dough, available at Greek and Armenian delicatessens. It is made from a batter poured through a perforated container onto a hot metal plate. In the process, the batter partially cooks into long strands resembling thin noodles or shredded wheat.*

Shredded Pastry Rolls / *Kadaife Rolo*

> Honey syrup (see below)
> 1 pound *kadaife* dough
> ½ pound almonds
> ½ pound walnuts
> ¼ cup sugar
> 2 teaspoons cinnamon
> ½ cup unsalted butter, melted

First make honey syrup (see below).

Remove *kadaife* dough from the package, and keep covered with clear plastic film to prevent it from drying out. Grind almonds and walnuts together, empty into a bowl, and mix in sugar, cinnamon, and 2 tablespoons water. Take a portion of *kadaife* dough about the size of a golf ball, and pat it out between your hands until it is about 3 inches wide and 4 inches long. Put a heaping teaspoon of the ground nut mixture at one end of the dough, and fold over the long sides of the dough; roll up and place on a lightly buttered baking sheet. Repeat. Brush the rolls with melted butter.

Bake in a 350° oven for 25 minutes, or until golden brown. Remove from oven. Using a slotted spoon, dip rolls into the cool honey syrup. Place on a platter. Serve when cooled to room temperature. Makes about 5 dozen.

HONEY SYRUP. Combine in a saucepan 1 cup water, 1 cup sugar, ½ cup honey, 2 teaspoons grated lemon peel, and 1 tablespoon lemon juice. Bring to a boil and simmer 5 minutes; let cool.

🦎

In this version, the nuts are layered between the shredded dough; then the pastry is cut into rectangles or diamonds.

Shredded Pastry / *Kadaife*

Honey syrup (see below)
1 pound *kadaife* dough
1 pound (4 cups shelled) walnuts, ground
½ pound (1½ cups shelled) almonds, ground
1 tablespoon cinnamon
½ cup sugar
1 cup unsalted butter, melted

First make honey syrup (see below).

Butter a 9-by-13-inch pan, and pat half the *kadaife* dough evenly into it. Mix together the walnuts, almonds, cinnamon, sugar, and 3 tablespoons water, and spread over the dough. Brush half the melted butter over the nut mixture, and pat remaining *kadaife* dough over the top. Brush the top with the remaining melted butter.

Bake in a 350° oven for 35 minutes, or until golden brown. Remove from oven and place pan on a rack. Pour the cool honey syrup evenly over the hot pastry. Let stand until cool, then cut into rectangles or diamonds. Makes about 3 dozen pieces.

HONEY SYRUP. Combine in a saucepan 1 cup water, 1 cup sugar, ½ cup honey, 2 teaspoons grated lemon peel, and 1 tablespoon lemon juice. Bring to a boil and simmer 5 minutes. Let cool.

This fila pastry was originated in 1863 to honor King George I, a Danish prince elected to the throne of Greece. A ground-almond sponge cake puffs up between fila layers; then all is saturated with a lemon-brandy syrup for another peerless fila pastry.

Almond Soufflé Pastry / *Kopehagi*

Syrup (see below)
8 eggs
1¼ cups sugar
2½ cups ground almonds
½ cup crushed zwieback crumbs
1 teaspoon baking powder
1 teaspoon cinnamon
½ cup unsalted butter, melted
12 sheets prepared fila dough

First make syrup (see below).

Beat eggs until thick and pale in color, and gradually beat in sugar; continue to beat at high speed until very thick, about 10 minutes. Mix together the almonds, crumbs, baking powder, and cinnamon, and fold into the egg mixture.

Butter a 9-by-13-inch baking pan and line with 6 sheets of fila, brushing each sheet lightly with melted butter and letting dough overlap sides of pan. Turn nut mixture into the dough-lined pan and spread evenly. Cover with 6 more sheets of buttered fila, tucking in the overlapping pieces of fila. Using a razor blade or sharp knife, cut through the top layer of fila, making lengthwise strips 1½ inches wide. Then cut diagonally, making diamonds.

Bake in a 350° oven for 50 minutes, or until golden brown and a knife inserted into the filling comes out clean. Remove from oven and cut into diamond-shaped pieces. Pour the cool syrup over pastry. Makes about 2 dozen pieces.

SYRUP. Combine in a saucepan 2 cups sugar and 1 cup water; bring to a boil and simmer 5 minutes. Remove from heat and stir in 3 tablespoons lemon juice and 3 tablespoons brandy or cognac. Let cool.

An almond soufflé expands within these slender fila rolls for a delicate, crispy finger pastry.

Nut Pastry Flutes / *Amigthalo Floyeres*

> 1½ cups finely ground almonds or walnuts, or half of each
> 2 eggs
> 1 cup sugar
> 1 teaspoon grated lemon peel
> 1 teaspoon cinnamon
> 18 to 20 sheets prepared fila dough
> ½ cup unsalted butter, melted
> Confectioner's sugar or (optional) syrup (see below)

Toast nuts in a 350° oven for 5 to 10 minutes, or until lightly browned. Beat the eggs until pale in color and thick. Gradually beat in the sugar, beating until stiff. Mix in lemon peel, cinnamon, and toasted nuts.

Lay out 1 sheet of fila (keep remainder covered with clear plastic film), and cut into thirds (making approximately 6-by-12-inch pieces). Brush with melted butter. Spoon a heaping teaspoon of nut batter over narrow end of dough, allowing a 1-inch margin around edges and base. Fold over long sides and bottom 1 inch. Roll up loosely and place seam side down on a lightly buttered baking sheet. Repeat. Bake in a 375° oven for 15 minutes, or until lightly browned. Transfer to a rack. Dust with confectioner's sugar while still warm. Or if desired, pour cool syrup over the hot pastries. Serve warm or cool. Makes about 4½ dozen.

SYRUP. Combine in a saucepan 1½ cups sugar and 1 cup water. Bring to a boil and simmer 5 minutes. Remove from heat and stir in 2 tablespoons lemon juice or brandy. Let cool.

❧

There are countless versions of halvah. The word denotes a ground sesame seed and honey candy, a baked cake with farina, and a sweetened, butter-browned cooked cereal, cut in diamonds. The latter follows.

Farina Diamonds / *Halvah*

½ cup butter
1 cup regular farina or cream of wheat
½ cup chopped almonds
1 cup water
1¼ cups sugar
2 cups milk
Cinnamon
Blanched almonds

In a large frying pan melt butter. Add farina and chopped almonds and cook over low heat, stirring, until lightly browned, about 10 minutes. Combine in a saucepan the water, sugar, and milk; bring to a boil and simmer 2 minutes. Slowly stir the syrup into the browned farina, and cook, stirring, until the liquid is absorbed. Pour into a buttered 9-inch-square pan and cool. Sprinkle with cinnamon, cut into diamonds, and garnish each piece with a blanched almond. Makes about 12 servings.

❧

This is a popular version of halvah served for dessert at the gay Athenian tavernas in the Plaka.

Farina and Nut Pyramid / *Halvah*

> 1½ cups sugar
> 2 cups water
> ½ cup butter
> 1 cup regular farina or cream of wheat
> ¼ cup chopped walnuts
> ¼ cup chopped almonds
> Cinnamon
> 2 tablespoons chopped pistachios

Combine the sugar and water in a saucepan, bring to a boil, and simmer for 2 minutes. Melt butter in a large frying pan, add farina, walnuts, and almonds, and cook over low heat for 10 minutes, stirring, until lightly browned. Slowly pour in the syrup and continue to cook, stirring, just until the mixture holds its shape. Spoon onto dessert plates, mounding in a pyramid. Sprinkle with cinnamon and pistachios. Let cool slightly and serve warm, or serve at room temperature. Makes about 8 servings.

This classic ground almond cake is light and delicate. With its diamond shape it is festive plain, or let it steep in a rum or lemon syrup.

Almond Cake / *Amigthalopeta*

> Rum or lemon syrup (optional; see below)
> 6 eggs, separated

⅛ teaspoon salt
⅛ teaspoon cream of tartar
1 cup sugar
⅓ cup zwieback or graham cracker crumbs
1 teaspoon baking powder
1 teaspoon grated lemon peel or orange peel
¼ teaspoon almond extract
2 cups finely ground almonds

First make rum or lemon syrup (see below) if desired.

Beat egg whites until foamy; add salt and cream of tartar, and beat until soft peaks form. Gradually add ½ cup of the sugar, beating until meringue stands in stiff peaks; set aside. With the same beater, beat the egg yolks until pale yellow in color, then gradually beat in the remaining ½ cup sugar, beating until thick and lemon-colored. Mix the crumbs with the baking powder and grated peel, and stir into egg yolks. Add the extract and half the almonds. Fold in the egg white meringue. Gently fold in remaining nuts, and turn into a buttered, floured 9-by-13-inch baking pan.

Bake in a 350° oven for 30 minutes, or until the top springs back when touched. While hot, if desired pour the cool syrup over cake. Cut into diamond-shaped pieces when cool. Makes about 3 dozen pieces.

RUM SYRUP. Combine in a saucepan 1 cup sugar, 2 teaspoons grated orange peel, 1 stick cinnamon, and ⅓ cup water. Bring to a boil and boil until clear. Remove from heat and stir in ¼ cup rum. Let cool.

LEMON SYRUP. Substitute 2 teaspoons grated lemon peel and ¼ cup lemon juice for the orange peel and rum in preceding syrup.

Nut cakes generally saturate a honey syrup, sometimes li-queur-flavored, but they are delicious without this extra sweetness. Pronounced car-ee-THO-pi-ta, this is a sponge cake type of walnut cake.

Walnut Cake / *Karidopeta*

> 6 eggs, separated
> 1 cup sugar
> ½ cup unsifted all-purpose flour
> 2 teaspoons baking powder
> 1 teaspoon cinnamon
> 1 teaspoon grated lemon peel
> ½ teaspoon salt
> 3 cups ground walnuts
> Honey syrup (optional; see below)

Beat egg whites until stiff moist peaks form. Gradually beat in ½ cup of the sugar, beating until stiff; set aside. Beat egg yolks until thick and pale in color; gradually add remaining ½ cup sugar, beating well. Stir together the flour, baking powder, cinnamon, lemon peel, and salt, and add to the yolk mixture, beating until smooth. Mix in half of the nuts. Gently fold the egg white meringue and remaining nuts into batter. Pour into an ungreased 10-inch tube pan.

Bake in a 350° oven for 35 minutes, or until a toothpick inserted comes out clean. Remove from oven, invert, and let cool in pan. When cool, if desired prick cake with a fine long wooden skewer, making holes about 1 inch apart, and slowly pour the hot honey syrup over cake. Remove from pan. Makes 16 servings.

HONEY SYRUP. Combine 1 cup sugar and ¾ cup water and bring to a boil; add ¼ cup honey and simmer 2 minutes. Remove from heat and stir in 3 tablespoons lemon juice or ⅓ cup rum.

🦁

The Greeks favor yogurt as a liquid ingredient in baking, letting it replace milk or cream. Here it contributes to a moist, tender nut cake, ideal for slicing thinly and eating out of hand.

Yogurt Cake / *Yiaourtopeta*

    1   cup butter
    1½ cups sugar
    4   eggs
    1   teaspoon grated lemon peel
    1   teaspoon cinnamon
    1   teaspoon vanilla
    1   cup yogurt
    2½ cups regular all-purpose flour
    1   teaspoon baking powder
    1   teaspoon baking soda
    ¼   teaspoon salt
    1   cup chopped walnuts

Beat butter until creamy and gradually beat in sugar. Add eggs, one at a time, and beat until smooth. Mix in lemon peel, cinnamon, vanilla, and yogurt. Stir together the flour, baking powder, baking soda, and salt, and add to the creamed mixture, beating until incorporated. Mix in nuts. Turn into a greased and floured 10-inch tube pan. Bake in a 350° oven for 1 hour, or until a toothpick inserted comes out clean. Let cool on a rack, then remove from pan. Makes about 16 servings.

※

Farina provides the flour and crunch for this syrup-soaked cake.

Baked Farina Cake / *Halvah Tou Fournou*

  1 cup butter
  1 cup sugar
  2 cups regular farina or cream of wheat
  6 eggs, separated
  1 teaspoon baking powder
  1 teaspoon cinnamon
  1 teaspoon vanilla
  ¾ cup pine nuts
  Syrup (see below)

Beat butter until creamy, and gradually beat in sugar and farina. Add egg yolks, one at a time, and beat well after each addition. Mix in baking powder, cinnamon, and vanilla. Beat egg whites until stiff peaks form, then fold into batter along with pine nuts. Turn into a greased and floured 9-by-13-inch pan.

Bake in a 350° oven for 35 minutes, or until golden brown and a toothpick inserted comes out clean. Remove from oven and pour the cool syrup over cake. Let cool completely. Cut into diamonds. Makes 36 pieces.

SYRUP. Place in a saucepan 2 cups sugar, 2 cups water, and 6 whole cloves. Bring to a boil and cook until sugar is dissolved. Remove from heat and stir in ¼ cup brandy. Remove cloves.

🦎

Short-grain rice is preferred for this custardlike pudding.

Rice Pudding / *Rizagalo*

⅓ cup short-grain rice
½ cup water
1 quart milk
2 tablespoons honey
⅛ teaspoon salt
3 eggs
½ cup sugar
1 teaspoon grated lemon peel
1 teaspoon vanilla
Cinnamon

Using the top of a double boiler, bring the rice and water to a boil over direct heat; cover and simmer until water is absorbed. Pour in milk and add honey and salt. Place pan over hot water, cover, and cook for 1 hour, or until rice is tender. Beat eggs until light, and blend in sugar and lemon peel. Pour part of the milk and rice mixture into egg mixture, and return to the double boiler. Stirring occasionally, cook over hot water until custard thickens. Remove from heat and stir in vanilla. Spoon into dessert dishes and sprinkle with cinnamon. Let cool. Serves 6.

🦎

This worldly "Mont Blanc" dessert is a familiar sight in Athenian pastry shops. The chestnut purée is piled high in metal sherbet dishes, garnished with swirls of whipped cream, and sprinkled with shaved chocolate or pistachio nuts.

Chestnut Purée Dessert / *Kastan Puree*

> 1 can (15½ ounces) unsweetened chestnut purée
> ½ cup sugar
> 1 teaspoon vanilla
> ¼ teaspoon salt
> 2 tablespoons brandy or cognac
> 1 cup heavy cream
> 2 tablespoons confectioner's sugar
> 1 ounce semisweet chocolate, grated

Place the chestnut purée in a mixing bowl and gradually beat in granulated sugar, vanilla, salt, and brandy, beating until smooth. Spoon into individual dessert dishes. Whip cream, and flavor with confectioner's sugar. Garnish dessert tops with whipped cream, and decorate with grated chocolate curls. Makes 6 servings.

CHESTNUT PIE VARIATION. Spread flavored chestnut mixture into a baked 9-inch pie shell. Cover with whipped cream and garnish with chocolate curls. Makes 6 servings.

🦎

Sophisticated tavernas *show off crêpes with a Greek flair like this:*

Orange Nut Crêpes / *Tiganites Yemistes*

> 16 crêpes (see below)
> ⅓ cup soft butter
> ½ cup sugar
> 2 teaspoons grated orange peel
> 3 tablespoons orange juice concentrate, thawed
> 4 tablespoons Grand Marnier or Cointreau
> 2 tablespoons Metaxa or cognac or brandy
> ⅓ cup toasted sliced or slivered almonds
> Fresh strawberries or orange sections

Fold crêpes in half, then in half again to form triangles. Beat the butter and sugar together until creamy. Beat in orange peel, orange concentrate, and 2 tablespoons of the Grand Marnier or Cointreau. Using a large frying pan or chafing dish over medium-high heat, melt the orange butter and heat until bubbly. Add folded crêpes to sauce, turning to coat both sides. Heat remaining orange liqueur along with Metaxa or brandy, ignite 1 tablespoon, and spoon flaming over the crêpes. Gently pour remaining liqueurs over crêpes and spoon sauce on top. Sprinkle each serving with nuts, and garnish with a few strawberries or orange sections. Serves 8.

CRÊPES. Place in a blender container 1 cup milk, 3 eggs, and ⅔ cup unsifted all-purpose flour. Cover and blend until smooth. Heat a 6-inch crêpe pan over medium heat, add ½ teaspoon butter, and tilt pan to coat surface. Pour in just enough batter to coat surface (less than 2 tablespoons), and quickly tilt pan to cover surface. Cook until golden brown on the edges and dry on top. Turn out onto a plate. (It is not necessary to cook both sides.) Stack crêpes and use immediately, or let cool and refrigerate up to 3 days. Makes about 16 crêpes.

🦂

Tuck these cookies into fluted paper baking cups when serving, as they shower powdered sugar when handled.

Sugar-Coated Butter Cookies / *Kourabiedes*

    1 cup unsalted butter
    3 tablespoons confectioner's sugar
    1 egg yolk
    ½ teaspoon almond extract
    ½ cup very finely chopped almonds, lightly
       toasted
    2 cups unsifted all-purpose flour
       About 2 cups confectioner's sugar

Beat butter until creamy, and beat in the 3 tablespoons confectioner's sugar, egg yolk, almond extract, and almonds. Mix in flour. Pinch off pieces of dough the size of a walnut and shape into rounds or crescents by rolling between the palms of your hands. Place on a lightly greased baking sheet. Bake at 325° for 40 minutes, or until lightly browned.

Remove from oven and let cool on the pan on a rack for 5 minutes. Sift a ⅛-inch-thick layer of confectioner's sugar over waxed paper and transfer cookies to it. Sift more sugar over the top to cover completely. Let stand until cool, then store in an airtight can. Makes about 5 dozen.

Athenian bakeries display this traditional Easter shortbread cookie in half a dozen shapes, such as rings, wreaths, pretzels, twisted fingers, and sticks.

Easter Shortbread Cookies / *Koulourakia*

½ cup unsalted butter
½ cup sugar
2 eggs
2½ cups unsifted all-purpose flour
2 teaspoons baking powder
¼ cup heavy cream
1 teaspoon vanilla
1 egg yolk beaten with 1 tablespoon milk
Sesame seeds

Beat butter until creamy, and gradually beat in sugar. Add eggs, one at a time, and beat until smooth. Stir together the flour and baking powder, and add to batter alternately with cream. Mix in vanilla. Pinch off portions of dough about the size of a walnut and roll on a lightly floured board into strands about ⅓ inch thick and 6 inches long. Fold in half and twist, twice, forming a twisted finger, or twist into a wreath, bringing the ends together. Place on a lightly greased baking sheet. Brush with the mixture of egg yolk and milk, and sprinkle lightly with sesame seeds. Bake in a 350° oven for 70 minutes, or until golden brown. Remove to racks and let cool. Store in an airtight container.

This version of twice-baked cookies, or Greek zwieback, is refined. In others oil and orange juice replace the butter; then the texture of the cooky sticks is coarse.

Sweet Biscuits / *Paximadia*

¾ cup butter
1 cup sugar
3 eggs
2 teaspoons crushed anise seed
1 teaspoon grated orange peel
3 cups unsifted all-purpose flour
1½ teaspoons baking powder
½ teaspoon salt
¾ cup coarsely chopped almonds

Beat butter until creamy, and beat in sugar. Add eggs, one at a time, and beat until smooth. Mix in anise seed and orange peel. Mix flour with baking powder and salt, and add to the creamed mixture, beating until smooth. Mix in almonds. Turn out on a lightly floured board and shape into 2 slightly rounded loaves about 3 inches wide and ¾ inch high and 16 inches long. Place on lightly greased baking sheets.

Bake in a 350° oven for 30 minutes, or until golden brown on the edges. Remove from oven and let cool 2 minutes. Slice each loaf in ½-inch-thick slices. Lay slices cut side down on the baking sheet and bake at 350° for 10 minutes longer, or just until golden brown. Let cool on racks. Store in an airtight container. Makes about 4 dozen cookies.

Oval cinnamon nut cookies bathe in honey syrup after baking.

Honey-Dipped Cakes / *Melomacarona*

½ cup butter
¼ cup olive oil
¼ cup sugar
1 egg
¼ cup orange juice
1 teaspoon grated orange peel
½ teaspoon cinnamon
2¼ cups unsifted all-purpose flour
1½ teaspoons baking powder
¼ teaspoon salt
1 cup very finely chopped or ground walnuts or
    almonds
Honey syrup (see below)

Beat butter until creamy. Add olive oil and sugar and beat until smooth. Mix in egg, orange juice, orange peel, and cinnamon. Stir together the flour, baking powder, and salt, and add gradually to batter, beating until smooth. Mix in ½ cup of the nuts. Pinch off small pieces of dough about the size of a walnut, roll into an oval about 2½ inches long and 1 inch wide, and place on a lightly greased baking sheet. Bake in a 375° oven for 20 to 25 minutes, or until golden brown. Transfer to rack and let cool. If desired, store in an airtight container until ready to serve.

To serve, with a fork dip cookies into the hot honey syrup, coating completely, and place on a serving plate. Sprinkle with the remaining finely chopped nuts. Makes about 3 dozen cookies.

HONEY SYRUP. Combine in a saucepan ¼ cup sugar and ¼ cup water, bring to a boil, and boil until clear. Add ¾ cup honey and heat until hot through.

🦎

Nut cookie balls, dipped in egg white and sugar, achieve a crackly sugar-crusted golden glaze after baking.

Almond Biscuits / *Amigthalo Biscota*

- ⅔ cup butter
- ½ cup sugar
- 2 egg yolks
- 1 teaspoon vanilla
- ½ cup ground almonds
- 1½ cups unsifted all-purpose flour
- 1 egg white
- Granulated sugar

Beat butter until creamy. Gradually beat in sugar. Add egg yolks and vanilla, beating well after each addition. Mix in nuts and flour, making a smooth dough. Pinch off small balls of dough and roll between the palms of your hands, making round flat balls about 1¾ inch in diameter and ½ inch thick. Beat egg white until frothy. With a fork, dip cookie dough rounds into the egg white and then in granulated sugar, coating completely. Place on a lightly greased baking sheet. Bake in a 350° oven for 20 minutes, or until golden brown. Transfer to a rack and let cool. Store in an airtight container. Makes about 3 dozen cookies.

🦎

Nut crunch makes a grand topping for ice cream or berries. Alone, it is a great candy as well.

Almond Praline / *Amigthalo Praline*

1 cup sliced or coarsely chopped almonds
1 tablespoon butter
¼ cup sugar

Place the sliced nuts, butter, and sugar in a large frying pan and heat over medium-high heat, stirring constantly, until nuts turn a golden brown. Turn out at once onto a buttered sheet of foil. Spread out evenly and let cool. Break into pieces or chop coarsely to use as a topping for ice cream or other desserts. Makes 1 cup praline.

During deep-fat frying this egg-rich dough blisters into bubbles all over its surface. As it cooks, you can quickly shape it into bow knots or curlicues.

Fried Honey Pastries / *Diples*

3 eggs
¼ teaspoon salt
1¾ cups unsifted all-purpose flour
2 tablespoons melted butter
Vegetable oil for frying
Honey
Cinnamon
Finely chopped walnuts or almonds

Beat eggs with an electric mixer until light. Add salt. Gradually add 1½ cups of the flour. Turn out on a board sprinkled with remaining flour and knead in the flour by hand. Knead in the melted butter, kneading until dough is smooth. Roll out a third of the dough at a time on a lightly floured board until as thin as possible (about ¹⁄₁₆ inch thick). Keep remaining dough covered with clear plastic film to prevent it from drying out. Using a pastry wheel, cut off strips about 1½ inches wide and 5 inches long. Cover strips with a tea towel to keep them soft.

Fry strips in hot deep fat at 375°, turning the strips with two forks into bow knots, curlicues, twists, or rolls. Remove when bubbly and golden but not browned. Drain on absorbent paper, then store in an airtight container. When ready to serve, drizzle with hot honey and dust with cinnamon. Sprinkle with finely chopped nuts. Makes about 4 dozen.

🐝

These deep-fat-fried "puff" balls are submerged in honey syrup and rolled in walnuts, thus the name luke-o-MOTH-es, which translates as "honey puffs."

Honey Puffs / *Loukoumades*

> Honey syrup (see below)
> 1 package active dry yeast
> ¼ cup warm water
> 1¾ cups milk
> ¼ cup butter
> ¼ cup sugar

½ teaspoon salt
3 eggs
4 cups unsifted all-purpose flour
Vegetable oil for frying
Cinnamon
Chopped walnuts

First prepare honey syrup (see below).

Sprinkle yeast into the warm water and stir until dissolved. Scald milk; pour into a large mixing bowl, and add butter, sugar, and salt; let cool to lukewarm. Stir in yeast mixture. Beat eggs until light and mix in. Gradually add flour, beating until smooth. Cover and let rise in a warm place until about doubled in size, about 1½ hours. Stir down dough. Dip out a teaspoon of dough at a time and drop into deep fat heated to 360°. Cook until golden brown, turning as necessary (it takes about 2 minutes). Drain on paper towels. While hot, dip into cool honey syrup, dust with cinnamon, and roll in chopped walnuts. Makes about 5 dozen.

HONEY SYRUP. Combine in a saucepan ½ cup water, 1 cup
   sugar, and 1 cup honey. Bring to a boil and simmer
   5 minutes.

This ultra-refreshing lemon ice has many serving possibilities. Mound it in cantaloupe half-shells or on wedges of honeydew. Or serve it in a dessert bowl ringed with strawberries and pass Cointreau to pour over. The King's Palace Hotel in Athens is famous for its lemon ice.

Lemon Ice / *Granita Lemoniou*

    2 cups water
    1½ cups sugar
    2 teaspoons grated lemon peel
    1 cup lemon juice

    Place water in a saucepan, add the sugar, and bring to a boil; cook until clear. Remove from heat and stir in lemon peel and juice. Pour into a shallow pan, such as a 9-inch cake pan, and freeze until set. Scrape into a bowl and beat with an electric mixture until thick and fluffy like cake batter. Return to a freezer container, cover, and freeze until solid. Makes about 1 quart, or enough for 6 servings.

In Greece it is proper to serve guests a tray with preserves, a glass of water with a spoon alongside, and a demitasse of Greek coffee or a liqueur. The guests sample a spoonful of the preserves. Thus they are often called "spoon sweets." This marmalade has a beautiful rich orange color, streaked with chewy peel throughout.

Orange Marmalade / *Marmelada Portocali*

> 8 oranges
> Water
> ½ cup lemon juice
> 5 pounds (approximately) sugar

With a sharp knife, score 6 of the oranges in quarters and remove peel. Place peel in a saucepan, cover with water, and simmer 30 minutes; drain. With a spoon scrape out any white pulp and strings. Cut peel very finely into julienne strips. Thinly slice the peeled oranges, and peel and slice the remaining 2 oranges. Place sliced oranges and the prepared peel in a large kettle. Add 1 quart water and the lemon juice. Cover and simmer 15 minutes. Weigh the fruit and juice and add an equal weight of sugar, about 5 pounds. Stir to blend, bring to a boil, and boil, stirring constantly for 10 minutes, or until jelly sheets from a spoon. Ladle into hot sterilized jars. Seal. Makes about 5 pints.

Sour red cherries make a delectable, tart preserve, and one that is favored on the tray for callers.

Cherry Preserves / *Vissino Glyko*

2½ pounds sour red cherries
4 cups (approximately) sugar
1½ tablespoons lemon juice

Wash and pit cherries, saving the juice. Weigh the cherries and juice, and place in a large kettle. Add an equal weight of sugar. Bring to a boil, stirring constantly, and boil, stirring and skimming off foam, until the liquid sheets from a spoon and forms a thick syrup. Add lemon juice, lower heat, and simmer 1 minute longer. Ladle into hot sterilized jars and seal. Makes about 6½ pints.

This is the old-fashioned way to make strawberry jam.

Strawberry Preserves / *Fraoules Glyko*

1 quart strawberries
4 cups (approximately) sugar
1½ tablespoons lemon juice

Wash and hull berries. Weigh the berries. Halve the large ones and place all the berries in a large kettle. Sprinkle with an equal weight of sugar and let stand half an hour. Place pan on a low heat and heat, stirring, until the sugar is dissolved and berries are juicy. Simmer over moderate heat about 15 minutes, or until the juice sheets from a spoon. Add lemon juice and simmer 1 minute longer. Ladle into hot sterilized jars and seal. Makes about 6½ pints.

🪶

A favorite pastime of the Greeks is to sit at the sidewalk cafés or coffeehouses, lingering over thick black coffee. It may be vary glyko (*strong and sweet*), metrio (*medium*), or sketto (*without sugar*). *This version is medium sweet.*

Greek Coffee / *Kafes*

4 tablespoons Greek coffee powder
2 teaspoons sugar
1 cup water

Place the coffee and sugar in a Greek or Turkish coffeepot and blend. Add the water and stir until well mixed. Place over moderate heat and bring to a boil. As soon as the coffee reaches the rim of the coffeepot, remove from heat and pour a little coffee into each demitasse-size cup (this is the froth of the coffee). Return pot to heat and let boil to the rim again. Pour coffee into each cup, being careful not to disturb the froth. Let coffee stand a few seconds before sipping to allow grounds to settle. Makes 4 servings.

INDEX

Index